Life at the Top

INSIDE NEW YORK'S GRAND HOTELS

BY

WARD MOREHOUSE III

Life at the Top

INSIDE NEW YORK'S GRAND HOTELS

BY

WARD MOREHOUSE III

BearManor Media
2005

Life at the Top: Inside New York's Grand Hotels
© 2005 Ward Morehouse III

For information, address:

BearManor Media
P. O. Box 750
Boalsburg, PA 16827

bearmanormedia.com

Cover design by Robert Antler of Antler Design Works

Typesetting and layout by John Teehan

Published in the USA by BearManor Media

ISBN—1-59393-034-8

To E.J.,

colleague and friend

TABLE OF CONTENTS

ACKNOWLEDGEMENTS

I'm indebted to the current and former owners and managers of a number of New York's Grand Hotels. Also, many of their employees, from bellboys to night managers, etc., have recalled for me the glamour of not only a bygone era but of today. Then, too, there are the celebrities and other VIPs who have shared some of their memories and reflections. The owners have included Stanley Bard of the Chelsea, the late Ben Bodne of the Algonquin, Kwek Leng Beng, co-owner of the Plaza for some seven years and head of Millennium Hotels, which owns and runs the Millennium Broadway Hotel and adjacent Hudson Theatre and conference center. Other industry leaders and hoteliers, in no particular order: Joseph E. Spinnato, president of the Hotel Association of New York City; Martin Riskin, who worked at the Waldorf, Plaza and Pierre; the late Seymour Durst; Andrew Anspach, manager of the Algonquin for many years; and Donald Smith, Ian Lloyd-Jones, Gunther Richner, Ivan Obolensky, Fred Gleason, Gary Shapiro, Tom Civitano, Gary Schweikert, Eric Long, Per Hellman, Paul Underhill, Richard Wilhelm, Ivana Trump, Donald Trump, James Blauvelt, Barbara McGurn, Barbara Lane, Larry Harvey, Robert Shanley, Robert Preston Tisch. Celebrities, who have taken the time to talk to me for this book as well as columns in the *New York Sun* and *am New York*, include Kitty Carlisle Hart, Jerry Lewis, Jerry Herman, Pete Hamill, Milton Glaser, George Lang, Amanda Burden, Vince Giordano, the late Cy Coleman, Barbara Carroll, Cindy Adams, EJ (Erin Jividen), David Romeo (composer of the musical *A Night at the Astor*), Tom Wolfe, Kathleen Landis, Paula Lawrence, the late Gary Stevens, Joey Reynolds, Danny Stiles, Joe

Franklin, Stewart F. Lane and Bonnie Comley. Also, Joel Pommerentz, Robert Dilenschneider, Richard Kosmicki, and Mary Francis Duffy. Editor Greg Collins, design consultant Bob Antler and publisher Ben Ohmart must be singled out for their considerable contributions. Also my agent Howard Sandum, who encouraged me to write about what I love. And special thanks to Craig Rosenthal, a co-author with me of *Eugene Walter and the Golden Age of American Theatre*, who helped with some of the research for this book. And many, many others.

PROLOGUE

A long time ago in a galaxy far, far away, this quaint ad appeared in the December, 1922, issue of *Theatre Magazine*:

DeSoto Hotel
Savannah, GA.
The Premier Tourist Hotel of the South
Open January 1ˢᵗ to May 1ˢᵗ
Modern and Luxurious in its Appointments, it Offers an Environment of Quiet and Refinement, Large Rooms, with Roomy Baths and Closets. Very Spacious Verandas. A Real Home for the Discriminating Tourist.

American Plan	**Unequalled**	Reduced Rates
Moderate Terms	**Winter Climate**	During January

Superior Roads for Automobilists. On the Scenic Routes of the South. Golf-Tennis-Hunting-Fishing. All Winter Sports. Booklets and terms sent on request.

J.B. POUND, President
SHERMAN DENNIS, Manager

Associate Hotels:
    Hotel Seminole   **Hotel Savannah**
    Jacksonville Fla.   Savannah, Ga.

Hotel Patten
Chattanooga, Tenn.

The Annex
Chattanooga, Tenn.

Summer Resort:
Monterey Hotel, Asbury Park, N.J.
Under the Same Management

My father was the renowned New York drama critic and Broadway columnist Ward Morehouse. His outlandish affection for hotels first started here, a long way from 42nd Street, at Savannah's well-fanned Victorian DeSoto Hotel, upon its spacious verandas and high in its castle-like tower. In his book, *Matinee Tomorrow*, my father wrote, "I don't know that taking to living in New York hotels and taking to prohibition gin contributed greatly to the Manhattanizing in my own case, but I do know that I had undergone, by 1925, something of a transformation: Some of my deep South politeness had vanished; I wasn't any quicker in movement…I had acquired something of the look-out-for-yourself-because-God-won't-do-it-for-you attitude." His outlook on life may have changed in the long hard journey from the Genteel South to Central Park South, but his fondness for hotel living never wavered.

Although I recollect accompanying my father to Savannah as a boy, by that time the DeSoto must have either been torn down or my memory of it fails me. I would, however, in the years to come more than make up for that lost time and that lost hotel. My own fascination with hotels may have started as a simple contagious reaction to my father's but soon I would be so in love with my own favorite hotels, namely The Plaza and The Waldorf-Astoria, that I suspect the poor DeSoto would have paled in my estimation.

My father, in fact, is the only person I know who might have given me a run for my money in love for hotels. He loved them so much he wanted to have "Room Service, Please!" inscribed on his tombstone. In his lifetime as an author, drama critic and playwright he stayed in hundreds of hotels around the world and lived in 29 in New York City alone. He kept a bear (a live one) at The Plaza and a raccoon at The Algonquin. I had a lion cub from South Africa at the old Seymour Hotel, next door to The Algonquin.

I got so used to hotels as a child that even now "home" is really a hotel room for me—despite my nice house in Connecticut, my cozy apartment in New York and my rustic Thousand Islands island up in Canada. My other "home" is the theatre. (I suppose it's fair to say my father's tastes had a big effect on me.) I remember on Saturdays as a kid sometimes seeing three and four shows—for a half hour each—then having a hard time telling friends why I'd seen so many. Hard at work making the rounds of the seemingly countless new shows back then, my father would deposit me in one and return in a half hour or so and we'd go to another. Of course, theatre life does run pretty deep in my family; ten other members have partaken in the theatre as producers, playwrights, actors and directors. My father's second wife, Jean Dalrymple, ran the New York City Center for 25 years when it was indeed America's first and only national theatre company.

"Our business is similiar to theater," Gary Schweikert, general manager of the Plaza, once told me. "It's setting the stage for people." So maybe my combined love for theater and hotels isn't so strange after all.

Some fathers boast to their sons of their war exploits or success in business or in sports. My father would tell me of the time he almost shot the hands off the Paramount Building clock from the window of his room at the Hotel Manhattan. At The Plaza, we'd light gunpowder in the sink and play a game in which he'd get into bed fully clothed wearing a wolf mask and then jump out growling when I came into the bedroom.

As a matter of record, I was *nearly* born at The Plaza, where my father and stepmother lived for eleven years. I say nearly because my parents resided there just *before* I was born. Then, *after* I was born, they moved to the Waldorf.

Some people think "living" at a hotel is strange. Or, at best, inconvenient. Like the proverbial child born in the theater trunk, it never bothered me. I've had, believe me, far rougher accommodations in my life. As a ten-year correspondent for *The Christian Science Monitor* I once lived with a tribe of Indians in the Amazon in order to produce a series of stories. I've also spent time in the upper reaches of the Canadian Arctic writing about Eskimos. As a Broadway columnist for the New York *Post* and later the "Broadway After Dark" columnist for the New York *Sun*, I saw my share of exciting times. I also had a lot of fun researching and writing my earlier books (both on New York hotels, naturally), *The Waldorf-Astoria: America's Gilded Dream* and *Inside The Plaza*.

But my peripatetic hotel-room childhood in New York City is almost certainly what set the stage for my own adventures later. Even my father's postcards were filled with the magic of the city, often reading like something out of *Peter Pan*.

"Dear Wardie," one began. "Do you remember those wild dogs and that engineer waving at you, and all the time Anna saying, 'No, Wardie, Don't Wardie?'"

Anna was my nanny, "from Hunger," as she used to say.

"I'll be back soon and will bring you a baby wolf," another letter began. "I also have your bat and ball and the gum bank, full of pennies. Here's some money for ice cream and stuff. With love, Daddy W."

There were thrilling telegrams, too: "Dear Wardie—Just a few more of these August anniversaries and you can have a bicycle and gun and ball and bat and you'll get into trouble with all of them as I always did. W.M."

One Christmas there was this telegram, "There's an island waiting for you and that belongs to you in the St. Lawrence whenever you're big enough to play in it. W.M."

The Island, and thankfully not the wolf, was literally true. It was one of the Thousand Islands and given to my mother at an American Theatre Wing benefit at the Waldorf-Astoria. (You knew there had to be a hotel connection in there someplace.) I've often thought of hotels as islands, self-contained but somehow never-ending cities of their own. Hotels have shops and restaurants and ballrooms and Broadway actors in the next room. Islands have coves and docks and outdoor fireplaces for cooking and entertaining. And when I became old enough and filled with enough curiosity to become a journalist myself, I became especially intrigued by Heart Island and its "Boldt Castle" because it was built by the man, George Boldt, who ran the Waldorf in New York, the old Waldorf on Fifth Avenue and 34th Street. How he got the island, whether he actually built it as a present for his wife or as a hotel on the St. Lawrence, was no matter. It was the mad adventure of the whole thing. That old musty northern castle was alive with New York, Fifth Avenue, trains, stations, glorious suites.

From their earliest days hotels have been pretty crucial as well as accommodating. We're told, after all, in the King James version of the Bible that since there was "no room at the inn," Joseph and Mary had to stay in a manger where the Lord Jesus was born. Of course, in those ancient days, the manger was really the bottom floor of a barn, where most guests stayed on tiers or balconies with the animals not far below. As inns evolved into full-fledged hotels, rooms at the top, farthest from the erst-while manger level, would become the most sought after.

The idea for this book about hotels grew out of my two previous books on the Waldorf and the Plaza. I had accumulated many entertaining stories that dealt with neither establishment. These random stories then began to assume a pattern, a portrait, if you will, of New York hotel celebrity and gossip. Certainly not the ultimate portrait but a colorful mosaic of hotel life leading up to and through the Twentieth Century nonetheless. Celebrity and gossip are the life's blood of hotels, it's what gives them their mystique, their legends. It's almost as impossible to separate the Astors and Vanderbilts and Boldts and Bemelmans from their hotels as it is to separate Liz Taylor or even modern day stars like Julia Roberts and Hugh Jackman from their movies. Moreover, at what point does a star's life end and the life of a hotel begin? In reality, there's no telling. The Carlyle, for example, is Woody Allen, who plays there on Monday nights with his Dixie Land Jazz Band, and Woody Allen is the Carlyle just as he is his movies.

Therefore, this book is not so much a narrative of progressive board-ing-house luxury in New York as it is an attempt to capture the personal-ity of the city's hotels through the eyes, ears and actions of its guests, its owners and its managers, some of them very famous, others not very. And all of them have one thing in common no matter which side of Park Avenue they are from. Whether it's Salvador Dali hosting a private dinner in the wine cellar of the St. Regis or Michael Douglas and Catherine Zeta-Jones sneaking into The Plaza to plan their wedding, people in ho-tels almost always—at least the interesting people—have a heightened sense of life and fun and, perhaps, although few want to face it, of their own mortality.

From John Jacob Astor IV, who built the St. Regis and the Astoria addition of the original Waldorf, to Ludwig Bemelmans, the flamboyant writer-artist and ex-banquet waiter who wrote about his exploits under fictional colors, the people who built, ran and lived in New York's hotels during the first half of the 20th Century were characters only George S. Kaufman and Moss Hart or perhaps Neil Simon could do justice to. I came to realize, to my astonishment, that there were few if any real chronicles of these fabulous hotels, all of which boast a social history as varied and as exciting, in my estimation, as the lore accompanying, say, The Palace Theatre or Winter Garden. And in New York during the 20th

Century, the theatre folk are the hotel people. The two are as inseparable as gin and tonic.

One extremely famous New York theater personality, Walter Winchell, lived in the penthouse of the St. Moritz (now the Ritz-Carlton) for many years. For those neophytes unfamiliar with Mr. Winchell, it will suffice to say that, during his heyday, a word in Winchell's column would help keep a play from closing even after the critics had murdered it. If he *really* liked something that had been panned it might even go on to become a hit. His St. Moritz penthouse was a duplex and afforded a priceless view of the most glamorous part of New York—Central Park and Fifth Avenue and Central Park West. This was the same apartment that *Hello Dolly!* composer Jerry Herman lived in and which he famously decorated all in white.

In his biography of Winchell, Neal Gabler relates that the uber-columnist kept a photo of a bloodied Barry Gray, the radio talk show host, on the wall of his St. Moritz penthouse. Despite his legendary run-ins with rivals like Gray or Lyle Stuart, who wrote an unauthorized biography of Winchell, Winchell had a high degree of respect for my father. As competing newspapermen they should have been rivals, but they got along swell. Maybe it was their mutual love of hotel life.

Over and over again, I've found that hotels make people dream again. Jerry Lewis was staying at the Waldorf Towers when I interviewed him in the Bull and Bear restaurant in December 2002. He said he was considering a return to Broadway even though he had serious health problems.

"I went to see *The Producers* last night," Mr. Lewis told me. "Such a wonderful show. My attorney called me and said there's a rumble in New York that Mel Brooks is looking for you to replace Nathan Lane. I said, 'I'm 76 years old, you schmuck! I can't do what they have in that show eight times a week!'"

Actors must be going soft. During the early part of the last century, the legendary Sarah Bernhardt lived at the fashionable Hoffman House on Broadway between 24th and 25th Streets, where she had a large suite. It was during the time she played "Hamlet" at the Palace Theater—with only one leg.

For New York City newspaper columnist Pete Hamill the legends surrounding some of the grand hotels, even those that have been razed, somehow survive. "There have been these figures (and hotels) which epitomized the era," he told me. "You know, Al Capone, Rosy Rosenthal and all the boring guys disappear. You know, no one gets nostalgic late at night about Robert F. Wagner. But they'll talk about Fiorello LaGuardia. Parts of New York are always dying. If you look at the turn of the century when all the big mansions were on Fifth Avenue, they're all gone. Ebbetts Field is not there...We're good at losing stuff. We know how to do that. I saw Penn Station go down. I don't mean by terrorism. That's unforgivable. But the sense of loss—life goes on. The best thing about us was September 12, 2001. People got up and went to work and had their kids...They didn't need politicians to tell them what to do. The hardhats came down the first night and said, 'We cut steel, you're going to need us.'...They had to come down to see if there was anybody beneath the broken steel."

"The loss of Penn Station was actually the impetus for the entire preservation movement in New York," famed artist and designer Milton Glaser told me. "It's a complex question in terms of planning, what you tear down and what you leave and it's attached to all kinds of emotional issues which have nothing to do with the health of the city."

For his part, Mr. Glaser doesn't have a favorite hotel per se. "It's funny, my nature is to be so eclectic. I don't have a favorite color or favorite food. I don't have anything. Everything is sort of contextual...The question of 'compared to what' always crops up."

Not all the changes have been bad. In Times Square, for instance, The Astor, a number of legitimate theaters, and many of the famous jazz hot spots disappeared with the square's rebirth which began slowly, agonizingly in the 1960s and has continued right up to the present day. One of the first positive changes in the area, though it wasn't a new office building or hotel, was Paley Park, named after former CBS Chairman William Paley.

"It really changed my life and it's very much a part of the family I come from," Amanda Burden told me. "When my stepfather, Bill Paley, built Paley Park (which boasted a mini-waterfall and clusters of tables for those who brown-bagged their lunch) I saw how that could really transform a street and give, in a small way, enormous pleasure to people. It was just a vacant lot before that."

As he turned 80 and could look back on 60 years in the hospitality industry, George Lang offered this assessment of New York's grand hotels as of June 2004:

"Some of the hotels, for example The Plaza, still deliver a wonderful quality. Restaurants in European hotels used to offer the best the cities could offer. And they have some of the finest, finest restaurants in hotels. The Savoy Grill in the Savoy in London and so forth. In the United States, it was just the opposite. There was no way to find a really good restaurant in a hotel. But that has changed drastically. I think that in the last ten years you have some wonderful restaurants in many of the hotels. The hotel restaurants, especially the new ones, they really care about quality."

Although he's much more of a restaurateur than a hotelier, Lang, who worked in both The Plaza and The Waldorf-Astoria, says guests "should feel the comforts and pleasures of their home without its problems." But he is quick to qualify this, saying, "If you want to please someone you must please them in their own way."

New York hotels have often become flash points for technical innovation in the country, from the St. Regis having primitive air-conditioning to the installation of the city's first passenger elevator in the Fifth Avenue Hotel.

Joseph E. Spinnato, President and CEO of the Hotel Association of New York City, is rightly proud of his association's 180 hotel members, including many of New York City's grandest hotels. Apart from the innovation of its members, The Association, founded in 1878, has received more than 15 communication awards.

But celebrity and humor, not dry statistics, will be the hallmarks of these pages. Hotels are full of people; and people, especially when they're far from home, are full of mischief. To wit, a couple of saucy appetizers before the main course:

Most elegant hotels proudly proclaim they cater to their guests' every whim. This is fine; however, when a guest's whim consists of a young blonde female knocking on his door late at night, problems can arise. Room Service is supposed to take care of guests' food and beverage wishes, with companionship not à la carte!

A clever concierge in one of New York's finest hotels had the bright idea of sending the requested lady to the guest's room bearing a chilled bottle of excellent champagne. For his work above and beyond the call of duty the concierge was richly rewarded by the guest, and then received a "gratuity" from the lady. When this procedure was discovered by the management, however, he was also rewarded with a pink slip, although he claimed the hotel always wanted to please its guests and he was just doing his job.

It has also been noticed generally that since a coin has two sides, an incorrect guess can cause quite a bit of trouble. Here's another example of a hotelier regrettably taking the wrong side:

In the lobby of a famous New York hotel for many years a number of chairs and couches were spread around for its guests and their friends. One evening a beautiful young lady entered the hotel and placed herself on a couch where she could observe everyone coming and going. When a security employee noticed the lady smiling at male hotel guests, he approached her and inquired if she was staying at the hotel. When her reply was "yes," he asked to see her room key. This infuriated lady refused and haughtily proclaimed she was Princess So-and-so. The security man, guessing she was a lady of the night, snapped at her saying: "Well, I'm the Duke of Windsor and you have to leave." The young woman rushed to the reception desk, insisting upon seeing the night manager. He came and confirmed that indeed she was Princess So-and-so as well as a guest in the hotel. The princess sued. The hotel lost the case, paying a substantial settlement. "The Duke of Windsor" was dethroned from his position at the hotel.

Royalty has caused more than its fair share of conundrums in New York's hotel lobbies. One day a gentleman approached the concierge of the St. Regis Hotel. In a loud voice he proclaimed: "Tell the princess, Count So-and-so is here." The concierge coolly—and earnestly—replied: "Which princess?"

That's New York hotels for you. You never know who you're going to run into, or get run over by, in the lobby. But now it's time to take our leave of the front desk to go up and inspect all those marvelous rooms.

CHAPTER 1

ROOM AT THE INNS

It was the last word in luxury, an unprecedented boon to technology, and hundreds of people from the five boroughs of New York City and miles around came to see it in all its glory. "It" was the city's first passenger elevator in the Fifth Avenue Hotel, which, when it opened in 1859 (it was completed in 1858) was swarming with pre-Civil War tourists as well as native New Yorkers. It was at the Fifth Avenue that Tom Platt, a Republican boss, wielded his political scepter in its "Amen Corner." Mr. Platt made a huge political miscalculation by supporting Teddy Roosevelt for Vice President of the United States—a cynical move intended to shipwreck TR's "higher" political ambitions. The trust-busting Roosevelt, instead of having his ambitious claws clipped as Veep, became President even sooner than he expected when President McKinley was assassinated in 1901. Roosevelt went on to become one of the greatest Presidents in history, to the great dismay of the country's power brokers, including Mr. Platt.

Before the Fifth Avenue Hotel's innovation, "vertical railways," or dumbwaiters, whisked up steamer trunks as guests walked up the stairs. "Eno's Folly," as the Fifth Avenue Hotel was called because it was so far uptown, was raised in 1908, the year after The Plaza was completed. A 15-story office tower, called appropriately enough, the Fifth Avenue Building, went up on the site of the old hotel. Built in 1856, Isaiah Rogers' six-story Astor House, on Broadway between Vesey and Barclay Streets, was the first hotel with plumbing above the first floor.

However, "long before Eno's Folly or the original Fifth Avenue, the first hotel in a modern sense, was the five-story, 137-room City Hotel, which opened in 1794," near Trinity Church,. so write Edwin G. Burrows and Mike Wallace in their Pulitzer Prize-winning book *Gotham*.

"Besides room and board, it offered facilities for public dining and dancing hitherto provided by taverns," the authors continue. "Its gracious accommodations and excellent wine cellars were especially designed to attract a wealthy clientele."

Likewise, the Pearl Street House, opening in 1810, catered to the wealthy. It was, the *Gotham* authors explain, intended specifically for commercial businessmen, not families or women.

Inns of the 1700s and early 1800s had been little more than taverns with some rooms above them. Historical indications are that luxury in the latter part of the 19th century, such as plumbing above the first floor and spacious single rooms, was nonexistent in most cases. One of the rules of these early inns, proclaimed:

> No more than five to sleep in one bed.
> No boots to be worn in bed…Organ
> Grinders to sleep in the wash house …
> No razor Grinders or Tinkers taken in.

It must be kept in mind that the notion of vacation travel was a relatively modern concept not only in America but the world at this time. First off, average people didn't get much vacation in the 19th century. Secondly, they couldn't afford travel anyway. This is an era in which most people never traveled more than a few miles from the places they were born. Travel was a necessity, almost exclusively, and then essentially for the rich. One of the first real "pleasure trips" in America was undertaken by a group of well-off Americans in the middle of the 19th century to visit the Holy Land. They chartered their own boat for this purpose, and a voyage to the places of the Bible no doubt struck their friends as less "frivolous." The voyagers were fortunate to number among them one Mark Twain, who wrote up the whole adventure in his first book, *The Innocents Abroad*, the first volume of pure "travel literature" in American letters and still the best.

Some of New York's hotels were actually country retreats. The Mount Vernon Hotel was constructed in 1799 as a carriage house for the William Stephen Smith estate. Perched on 26 acres of what is now pricey East 63rd Street between York and First Avenues, the carriage house was converted into a small hotel—more like a boarding house, really, than a hotel—in 1826. A boarding house "lessens the necessity of marriage," said James Silk

Buckingham, a prominent English lecturer of the time. It afforded conviviality, comfort and good food, which are some of the hallmarks of marriage, or at least are supposed to be. Today, the one-time hotel is run by the Colonial Dames of America as a museum. When it was a hotel, some wayfarers spent the night in spacious high-ceilinged rooms but largely, large gentlemen of means spent the day there much as their modern day counterparts do at country clubs. They played cards, drank and discussed the news of the day. In fact, long before the original Waldorf helped provide the ultimate alternative to the private gilded ballrooms of the rich and privileged, Daniel Webster, the great scholar and orator, was married (for the second time) in the Eastern Hotel. Jenny Lind, the operatic sensation called "The Swedish Nightingale," once graced its suites and dining room.

Hotels in New York have never strayed very far from the theater world. And, just as they did on Broadway nearly a century later, the theaters, which had cropped up around City Hall Park, attracted the seedy sex parlors of that day. There was, after all, something unavoidably salacious about both the concepts of watching women prance around a stage and of staying somewhere away from home—where, golly, a person might do just about anything. Hotels were a major part of the onset of American social freedoms, of finally getting off the farm, and away from the nosy neighbors. Anything in that era that did not take place either at home, at church, or at the workplace was naturally assumed to be scandalous. And, of course, often was. Even the pioneers took their whole families and households with them when trekking across the country. The Pilgrims transported not only their wives and children, but their livestock, when they came across the Atlantic. Traveling someplace just for "fun" was a downright wicked, self-indulgent, extravagant notion.

"Theater owners, including John Jacob Astor, who had purchased the park (City Hall Park) in 1806 encouraged erotic third tiers (theater balconies) as drawing cards, providing special entrances through which the ladies of the evening could enter," according to *Gotham*. Much later, in the 1960s, prostitutes lived at a ramshackle hotel on Sixth Avenue and 44th Street, just East of the Belasco Theatre. They would try to cull clients from those who had purchased tickets in the Belasco balcony. Ladies of the evening chased the late Times Square developer Seymour Durst down 44th Street when he threatened to raze some of their old haunts. The Belasco, by the way, was once the longtime home of *Oh, Calcutta!* Much later, both comedies and dramas, like the production of *Hamlet* starring

Ralph Fiennes, and *Enchanted April* with Elizabeth Ashley and Jayne Atkinson, graced its stage. My mother appeared in the play *Mr. and Mrs. North*, a detective story, which later became one of the first TV series.

As is evident throughout this book, New York hotels and New York theater have been close companions. Songwriter Irving Berlin and my father took what my father called "a sentimental journey" to Manhattan's Lower East Side where Berlin lived as a child. Berlin was 58 years old and living in a posh townhouse. And Berlin, who often stayed in some of America's swankiest hotels where he'd write songs well past midnight, became animated when the chauffeur-driven car they we in reached the intersection of the Bowery and Bayard Street. "Over three," Berlin said excitedly, pointing to the other side of the thoroughfare, "was the Cobdock Hotel, a flop house…No, it would have resented being called that. it was a place to which the gals would take their sailors…I remember a barroom at Nov. 23 run by a fellow named Sisto and No. 9 was a terrible joint, inhabited by the drunkest sailors and the oldest hags. I also went there and passed the hat. A lodging house called the Mascot was right near where Bayard runs into the Bowery and I lived there for a year. it was a 15-cents-a-night joint. You got a cubby hole to sleep in, one open at the top, and you were always scared that somebody would reach over and steal your pants!" Later, that same evening after returning from the Lower East Side, Berlin added, "America has been very good to me. I am very proud and grateful to live in a country where it's possible to do what you like. The toughest thing about success is that you've got to keep on being a success. Talent is only a starting point in this business."

Nathan Silver writes in *Lost New York* that hotels were originally inns which attempted to provide satisfactory food and comfortable shelter for travelers. But places like the Fifth Avenue Hotel and the Netherland, which once occupied the site of the current Sherry-Netherland, offered ambience and grandeur as well as comfort. "Prosperous New Yorkers found that they did not need to maintain town residences if social standing was equally assured at certain levels" in hotels, Silver writes.

The Oriental and Manhattan Beach Hotels were ornate wood-frame palaces in the Coney Island section of Brooklyn, "when that part of Brooklyn was still a long day's trip away from downtown New York," the author notes.

Ironically, during the bloody Civil War, "The great hotels were glittering and crammed. Hundreds of contented Republican males packed the Astor House's smoke-filled, gas-lit Rotunda for evening expeditions… After 1862, they would dine at Lorenzo Delmonico's latest and most luxurious restaurant, in the converted Moses Grinnell mansion at Fifth and 14th, one block west of Union Square," *Gotham* relates. Delmonico's would later have a branch on Fifth Avenue at 44th Street near the Hotel Mansfield, built in 1904 as a hotel for upwardly mobile gentlemen, and which in recent years has been renovated.

And, yes, New York was moving uptown. Union Square and Madison Square were prosperous. Townhouses and hotels sprang up there in great profusion at a time when upper Fifth Avenue and Central Park West played host to cow pastures and swamps, with farms and the occasional tavern. As time went on, armories played a big role in the march of hotels and townhouses and more ostentatious mansions uptown. They were not so subtle reminders of who was in charge that stood sentinel for the rich amid the poorer masses huddled in their "railroad" flat tenements east of Park Avenue. New York City hotels had already given us the first passenger elevator and helped lead the fight for universal indoor plumbing. The Hotel Association of New York City was actually formed in 1878 to help lobby for indoor plumbing.

Lloyd Morris, is his book *Incredible New York*, talks about this astounding transformation taking place in Manhattan's commercial life. He says as the second half of the 19th century dawned, "People were awed by the splendor of its (Manhattan's) hotels and theaters, its costly, magnificent stores."

In the 1880s Chelsea, which has in recent years regained tremendous popularity as one of Manhattan's most coveted residential neighbors, boasted the cream of society. Built on a scale only equaled on Madison or Union Squares, the Chelsea Hotel opened as an exclusive apartment house in 1882. It was designed by architect Philip G. Hubert, who built several ornate multi-family dwellings in prosperous areas like Fifth Avenue in the 50s near St. Patrick's Cathedral. It wouldn't become a hotel until 1905, the year after the St. Regis opened. And while its physical interior accoutrements have long been outshined by countless relative newcomers, its celebrity status has shown brighter with each passing year with tales of Thomas Wolfe, Dylan Thomas, Brendan Behan, Jackson Pollock and countless other artists.

However, it was really The Waldorf Hotel, which opened in 1893 (the same year as Quebec's castle-like Frontenac Hotel), that began to establish hotels as America's unofficial palaces. Likewise, George Boldt, who had once been a poor migrant dishwasher, created a standard for service with his oft-repeated adage, "The customer is always right," a sentiment that challenged European traditions of luxury. He eventually came to live almost as princely as the Astors.

According to Roger S. Lucas in a short history of The Bellevue-Stratford Hotel, it was one Abner Barlett from New York, an advisor to William Waldorf Astor, who suggested that Astor hire George C. Boldt to run his New York hotel (which had been christened with Mr. Astor's middle name). Boldt, already a veteran hotelier, saw the potential of managing The Waldorf but sweetened his own compensation considerably by insisting on a profit-sharing plan, Mr. Lucas says. Boldt not only became wealthy, he developed a proclivity for grand estates which rivaled and, in one case, almost exceeded those of his boss. Boldt is the gentleman who built that castle on Heart Island in the Thousand Islands region of The St. Lawrence River near Alexandria Bay—at a cost of $3 million, before work came to a sudden halt when his wife died.

Like theaters, fine restaurants were magnets for hotels. Delmonico's restaurant actually had seven locations over the years. Its uptown location at 44th Street and Fifth Avenue not only helped Fifth Avenue become fashionable but became, along with the McKim, Mead and White-designed Sherry's restaurant, an anchor on the side street of 44th Street, leading to the construction of fine clubs and hotels, including the New York Yacht Club and the Mansfield Hotel.

Delmonico's Hotel at 58th Street and Park Avenue was a favorite of many celebrities. The Beatles stayed there on one of their trips to New York following their initial stay at The Plaza Hotel in February 1964. Well-known art consultant Luisa Flynn has lived there for many years after giving up her townhouse on East 92nd Street. When she was selling her townhouse, Al Pacino was one of those interested in snatching it up. He even came up to the house to get "the feel" of what it would be like living in a house versus an apartment. "Go to the top of the stairs and I'll go outside and come in and say, 'Honey, I'm home!' he told Mrs. Flynn. After all this was said and done, however, friends convinced him to stick with an apartment in midtown to remain near, among other things, his all-night delis.

Five hotels, the Hotel Wales, the 160-room Washington Square Hotel on Waverly Place (which opened as the Hotel Earle), The Algonquin (which opened in 1902) and the Martha Washington on East 29th Street, have the distinction of being the oldest hotels in New York.

The fifth, The Chelsea Hotel, built in 1882 as an upscale apartment house, was not converted into a hotel until 1905. But in the last 100 years it may have housed more talented and eccentric people than any other structure on earth. So many in fact that it requires a separate chapter to accommodate them all.

CHAPTER 2

THE CHELSEA HOTEL

In the fateful year of 1912, the Hotel Riverview at 113 Jane Street took in a number of *Titanic* survivors after they were brought to New York aboard *The Carpathia*. Most of those who stayed at the Riverview were from steerage, but the first class passengers were put up at the Chelsea, which had been converted into a hotel only seven years earlier.

The Chelsea Hotel, built two years before the Dakota in 1882, is largely synonymous with Stanley Bard, its proprietor. Or rather, it represents the qualities of encouragement, forbearance and love Mr. Bard and his father before him expressed running the world's most artist-friendly hotel.

Mr. Bard, who might have been right at home conducting a symphony orchestra, is a conductor of sorts for his guests, who range from the rich and infamous to the talented and unknown on their way to possible stardom in their respective fields.

"There's hardly an artist in this city or maybe in the world that didn't, at one time or another come and stay here," Mr. Bard, a pleasant looking, relaxed man told me over coffee one morning in his office at the red-brick Chelsea, which like the lobby, is festooned with art and sculpture. "Or that the Chelsea at one time or another didn't embrace. House them. You know, if you're interested in the artist it is a beautiful place to be. The Dakota was the oldest apartment building and the Chelsea was the oldest hotel—although when it was built in 1882 it was an apartment house."

The Chelsea, on West 23rd Street between 7th and 8th Avenue, became a hotel in 1905, with Mr. Bard's father assuming control of it in 1939. Over the years it became home, both temporary and permanent, to William S. Burroughs, Virgil Thompson, Tennessee Williams (who eventually preferred the more elegant Elysee on East 54th Street where he died choking on a cough syrup bottle cap), Thomas Wolfe, Bob Dylan, Robert Mapplethorpe and a veritable Who's Who of artists, writers and musicians. In sheer numbers, they overshadowed those artists associated with The Algonquin, like James Thurber and Robert Benchley. But the Chelsea was and is radically different from the Algonquin. Artists who favor the Chelsea are for the most part employed only by themselves; those at the Algonquin often work for someone else, for newspapers and magazines— that is, they have actual "jobs."

"I came here in 1941 as a child to see my father," Mr. Bard said. "He was a workaholic. That caused me a lot of stress…I went to the opening of Arthur Miller's *A View from the Bridge*, which had recently opened at the Metropolitan Opera. It really was so exciting for me because the entire concept almost was born here in the Chelsea Hotel and Arthur collaborated with two of my tenants here to do it. Bill Maddin wrote the music and Arnold Weinstein did the lyrics with Arthur. And this concerned the whole project, which first opened in the Chicago Opera House. I saw first hand this love they had for the project. I was happy for them and excited being there [at the Met] with them. So many things started here in this hotel. It's almost unreal that one institution like the Chelsea Hotel would have attracted all these wonderful creative people…It feeds on itself."

Built on an upscale level for its time, it rivaled the Dakota, for esteem, Mr. Bard said.

After having lived in Brooklyn and on First Avenue in the 40's, Thomas Wolfe settled in to the Chelsea Hotel in the late 1930s where he did some of his finest writing, often at night. It was at the Chelsea that Wolfe was also able to get away from the professional apron strings of editor Max Perkins and Scribners Publishing House. In fact, he signed a contract with Harper's for his next novel. Edward C.C. Aswell, an assistant at Harper and Brothers, hand-delivered a $2,500 advance on that next novel to Wolfe at the Chelsea. Wolfe wrote, biographer Donald reports, that he had a "strangely empty and hollow feeling" in signing the contract. "Yet," Wolfe added, "A new world was before me."

Shedding some light on Wolfe's writing habits at the Chelsea, Mr. Donald says, "Most of the time while Wolfe was working on a new book he followed a regular routine. He continued to get up late in the morning, and he usually started writing without having any breakfast, though he occasionally sent down to the hotel lobby for coffee. He worked until about five or six o'clock, when he would break for a drink. After a large dinner…he usually went back to his rooms and continued what he was writing. He usually worked until after midnight, tormented, he confided, that 'he can't stop thinking about it.'"

Max Perkins, Wolfe's editor at Scribners, wrote in an introduction to an edition of *Look Homeward Angel* that the author's humble quarters at the Chelsea and other New York apartments, "always looked as if he had just moved in, to camp for awhile. This was partly because he had no real interest in possessions of any kind, but he was in his very nature a Far Wanderer, bent upon seeing all places, and his rooms were just necessities into which he never settled."

While Wolfe would make due with a table and refrigerator, other artists transformed their apartments into something more lavish. Martin Riskin, a hotel executive who worked at the Pierre, St. Regis and Plaza before starting his own wine-importing business, remembers visiting Virgil Thompson at the Chelsea.

"He had excellent tastes," Mr. Riskin told me. "And he was one of the most cultured and refined people I have ever met in my life…Virgil was a very important person. He felt there was artistry in the old hotel…He was the kind of person, his art was supreme…He could compose there without the hustle and bustle of The Pierre or the St. Regis."

In the book, *Hotel Chelsea*, theater poet Arnold Weinstein name-drops like only someone living at the Chelsea could: "I got dressed in a black shirt, [to go out and] to meet the finest Euro trash the music world could buy. Never got past the 23rd Street subway entrance. I had a better shot at royalty back home at the Chelsea Hotel. In the lobby where a year earlier I had read the book I co-wrote with Larry Rivers, who lived next door to Arthur Miller my co-writer of the libretto, *View from the Bridge*, I bumped into Prince Hal Willner who produced a record of my translation of a song by Brecht whose son [lived] next to the Duke and Duchess of Renfry …"

And so it goes from Warhol ex-superstar Viva to Herbert Hunche, who Mr. Weinstein said coined the word "beat."

Life at The Chelsea took unexpected turns for poet-photographer Gerard Malanga after meeting Edie Sedgwick of Warhol Factory fame. He writes in *Hotel Chelsea* that "after meeting her in 1969 at a restaurant in St. Mark's Place…we hail a cab and shoot over to the Chelsea Hotel, ascend to the 5th Floor…smoke a 'j' and suddenly end up in each other's arms under the covers...In the morning, I quietly slip out of bed, dress, glance over at Edie fast asleep...It's the last time I would see her alive ..."

Pete Hamill, the columnist and author, lived at the Chelsea nearly two years. "I stayed at the Chelsea Hotel a couple of times," he told me. "Down the block is the Flatiron Building. It's still there. If these guys take out the Woolworth Building, then I say kill their mothers. You know, kill everybody, if they do that."

Did he get any special inspiration living at The Chelsea? "Not really," he said. "By then, I always knew it was temporary. Until I found a place that I really wanted. I stayed for a year one time and another time for about six months. But I liked it. I liked some of the people there. Stanley Bard. And I liked 'the hustle.' Some kid would come in with a guitar and say, 'I want to stay where Bob Dylan wrote "Tambourine Man."' 'Oh, let me see what's empty. 601.' And they would send him up. I loved that part of it."

Actor-director Ethan Hawke came to the hotel to find more of the artist within himself. "He had done this movie digitally, which was done for the first time," Mr. Bard recalled. "Ethan said there was something in this building that's unexplainable. Things happen within these walls. Ethan tried to portray that in his movie, make the walls talk. People were talking to the walls as a sounding board and the walls were talking back. There's something in these walls maybe because the past greats who worked here left their mark, something that makes the young people who come here believe their dreams are more real. This informality, this peacefulness, this quietness, this camaraderie...It's many things put together...My wife always says a place has a heart and a soul ..."

Of course, artists sometimes do have their temperamental side: "I made Brendan Behan understand what he could do and not in the hotel. Dylan Thomas kept to himself. Thomas Wolfe kept to himself. When they were drinking, they drank but kept to themselves. Brendan was not that way. Brendan wanted to be loud, noisy and heard. He was what you'd call not a very good drinker and he caused a lot of trouble which I heard about...I knew his publisher who was trying to get him to finish his two books. Ironically, he finished those two books here. And I often had people who, if they wanted to complete something and couldn't, they would complete it at the Chelsea.

"But Brendan knew I wouldn't tolerate destructiveness and respected that part. I think Brendan knew and understood what I would expect of him while he was here. I couldn't stop his drinking. No one could. But I could stop his being destructive. And he stayed. Stayed for a year. He brought his wife over. Beatrice, from Ireland. And he did finish his two books here. And we did have our moments where we had this confrontation. He stayed until he did finish his two books and wanted to go home. His wife was pregnant and went home and had a child."

Dylan Thomas, whose legendary American tours took him from his beloved Wales, would not be as lucky as Behan. After one binge, the writer of "Under Milkwood" and other classics fell into a coma at the Chelsea Hotel on November 4, 1953 and died November 18 at age 39. He left his wife Caitlin and three children in Wales. His many poetic protestations of love to Caitlin, such as "Caitlin my own dearest love," were silenced.

Like his father before him, Mr. Bard has "always been very, very prone to helping arts and the artist. And I continue that. In fact, one of my former tenants, Christo, recently got the go ahead to do one of his installations in Central Park. And Christo attributes where he is today to my understanding in helping him and his family which came from Europe when he didn't have any money at all and I allowed him to stay at the hotel. I trusted him and he never forgot that."

Did Mr. Bard sense Christo would become an artist of note? "Yes, he had ideas that were very unique and avant garde."

Today, Stanley Bard's son, David, is managing director of the hotel; the third generation of Bards to run The Chelsea.

Theater and burlesque impresario and artist Norman Gosney has lived in the penthouse of the Chelsea. He told me in 2003 that "about twelve years ago I got paid by Dick Clark. He had a project that he thought might fit into the Chelsea. He paid me to check out all the rumors of what bands stayed there. I was amazed. They *all* stayed there. I got a friend who was born in the hotel and the first memory he comes out with is that Janis Joplin had a strawberry, a birthmark! And his *next* memory if of being in Janice Joplin's arms and looking up and touching her strawberry."

CHAPTER 3
THE ALGONQUIN HOTEL

In the beginning there were the Indians, the Algonquin Indians. They roamed the land from the Hudson River to the East River and beyond. Forty-fourth Street was a footpath and part of it heavily wooded. The Algonquin Hotel opened in 1902—a time when 44th Street had become a well worn footpath for a different type of New York native. It was a hotel for well-to-do bachelors and actors, both gainfully employed and unemployed, and quickly became a kind of boarding house for some of the most notable names in the theater, from John Barrymore to playwright Eugene Walter. The latter struck it rich with some of the century's first realistic plays, megahits of the day such as *Paid in Full* and *The Easiest Way*.

But it's the Algonquin Round Table that has put the hotel indelibly on the American map. The legend of the Round Table has endured through the decades with a vigor and fascination greater than its individual parts. The informal luncheon club was frequented by, among other theater and literary luminaries: Alfred Lunt and his wife Lynn Fontaine, Alexander Woollcott, George S. Kaufman and Edna Ferber. Alfred and Lynn were the Lunts, the celebrated stage acting couple. Woollcott, rotund drama critic of *The New York Times*, was the prototype for Sheridan Whiteside in the Kaufman-Moss Hart comedy, *The Man Who Came to Dinner*. Edna Ferber wrote the novel *Showboat*, which was later adapted into a rather well-known musical of the same name. Dorothy Parker also would drop by for lunch on occasion. If her famous (and premature) epitaph for Katherine Hepburn's stage emoting—her acting "ran the gamut of emotions from A to B"— didn't originate at the Round Table, at least legend has it that way and it is legend that keeps the Round Table alive 75 years after it was disbanded.

New Yorker scribe Wolcott Gibbs reports the Round Table was dissolved in 1929 because members had become so famous individually they had little time for each other as a group. Woollcott "moved their poker game from The Algonquin to the Colony where the check for refreshments was usually more than anybody had made in a week when the Round Table began," Gibbs added.

Humorist James Thurber, although he loved staying at the Algonquin, which was across from the *New Yorker* magazine's editorial offices where he worked, had disdain for the remnants of the Algonquin Round Table. In his biography of Thurber, Burton Bernstein says *New Yorker* editor Harold Ross took Thurber and fellow star writer E.B. White to the Roundtable and he didn't like it a bit. "Thurber and I were much younger than most of the others," White said in Burnstein's book, "and everything they said seemed so rehearsed."

People, like my father, who was never part of the intimate circle— "the vicious circle," as Dorothy Parker called them—somehow became linked in the public's mind with the group. Meanwhile, John Barrymore's tenancy at The Algonquin began long before the Round Table came to full flower in the mid-1920's.

The Algonquin was a lot more than a hotel to many of its illustrious patrons and Barrymore fit this category. Outside of his Hollywood Hills aerie, purchased largely with money he made from *Richard III* and other silent movies, The Algonquin may have been the Great Profile's most beloved home. Frank Case became, in the absence of his own father—the mercurial Maurice Barrymore—John Barrymore's surrogate father. Case, in his 1943 book, *Do Not Disturb*, a sequel to his earlier autobiography, *Tales of a Wayward Inn*, tells of his shock to read in *Who Tells Me Time*, a book by Michael Strange, Barrymore's second wife, of the dark side of the Great Profile. "Michael Strange tells of a Barrymore," Case relates in *Do Not Disturb*, "I never knew, for the youth I knew was gay, witty and terribly amusing."

In 1940, When Barrymore was starring in his final Broadway show, *My Dear Children*, a vehicle that showed his worst profile, quite figuratively, Case began thinking back to when he saw Barrymore in another play before he'd gone to Hollywood to become both rich and a confirmed drunkard.

"Perhaps it was a matinee, perhaps business was not at capacity," Case recalled. "In either case, I was able to get an aisle seat well down in front, second or third row where the Profile did not discover me until the second act was well under way."

Barrymore, Case related, was on stage dictating a letter to his secretary in the play.

"Fixing a malevolent eye under a bent brow on me," Case relates, Barrymore ad-libbed, 'Take another letter. Dear landlord—not this week, perchance not next week, but [long pause] anon!'"

Actually, Case felt that Barrymore and other actors were generally good credit risks. "People of the theater—if not today, some other day. In a talk with Frank McIntyre at The Lambs, I made the statement that I had never lost a nickel by nonpayment of a bill by an actor when Frank interrupted with, 'What a lie! How about George Lifeless?' naming a lad who hadn't done exactly right by me and quite extensively.

"Yes, but would you call him an actor?" Case asked.

"You win again," ceded McIntyre.

When Case found guests irate about one thing or another, as they inevitably were, he tried to call upon inner reserves of unruffled calm—especially if it involved an employee.

"Unless Mary, the maid on my floor is discharged, I shall leave the hotel," one irate guest once accosted Case.

"We shall be very sorry to lose you, Mrs. Guest," Case tearily replied.

"Do you mean to say that you would let *me* go rather than discharge a *servant*?" the thunderstruck guest rejoined.

"Well, you see there are 130,000,000 potential guests in the United States alone, not counting Europe and Canada, but a really good chambermaid isn't found every day," Case replied, adding that Mary stayed on and Mrs. Guest stayed on, too, for years and years, and they became good friends.

"Humorist James Thurber's first meeting with Robert Benchley occurred at Benchley's apartment at The Algonquin. He was picking up Benchley's 'copy' for the *New Yorker* and the two sat down for some serious drinking until the *New Yorker* called to ask what had become of Thurber and Benchley's copy!"

On the eve of his 55th birthday, Thurber said in an interview at The Algonquin, where he maintained an apartment, "Man will not get anywhere until he realizes, in all humility, that he is just another of God's creatures, less kindly than the Dog."

As the 1920's roared with the boom of the stock market, Broadway and Babe Ruth, there entered, unobtrusively from stage left, a 24-year-old

Benjamin Bodne and his wife, who would lovingly preserve the chief New York hangout of such super celebs as tennis great "Big" Bill Tilden and writers Sinclair Lewis and F. Scott Fitzgerald until nearly the next century.

Bodne loved baseball, travel and The Algonquin and from 1946, when he bought the hotel that Woollcott, Dorothy Parker and James Thurber built on their wits more than their dollars, he lived modestly but comfortably in a huge apartment on the 10th floor of the hotel. I interviewed him just months before he died in his apartment and he told me the same story about my father that he had on several other occasions.

"Your father said he wanted me to see, *Edward, My Son* in London," Bodne recollected. "I thought Ward meant he had a *son* in London. He was talking about the play with Robert Morley."

"Friends of the hotel were appalled that the future of New York's most sophisticated hotel had been entrusted to a rube," one magazine writer said of Mr. Bodne's takeover of The Algonquin.

In fact, that there has even been a second half century of history of The Algonquin is because the short, powerfully built former Texas oil man Bodne purchased the hotel in 1946 for $1 million—more than five times what Frank Case paid for it 18 years earlier. Bodne, in turn, sold it for $19 million in 1986 while continuing to have use for life of that cavernous apartment on the 10th floor. The Bodne suite took up much of the 10th floor of the hotel—a big "U." One corner was filled with luggage as if they'd just returned from a trip or were soon going on their next one. That last time I interviewed him, after he'd repeated the same stories he always told me about my father, I filled him in on what I was doing—I'd just done a book on The Waldorf-Astoria. Whenever I spoke to Ben Bodne, I always got the feeling I was talking to a baseball manager type, a Casey Stengel—few frills and airs but decency and common sense—with some humor. Mr. Bodne and his wife smiled easily. Their health wasn't the best by this time but they'd really enjoyed their lives at the hotel and traveling that other world outside the hotel.

"Bodne, who claimed he was playing semi-pro baseball by the time he was 16, had grown up poor in Charleston, South Carolina, only to return to operate that city's first deep-water oil terminal," *New York* magazine reports. "By the end of World War II he was ready to get out of oil and buy himself a baseball team. Bing Crosby had gotten the Pirates first. The Yankees were not for sale. So it was left for the squatish, graying middle-age Bodne, his wife and two daughters, to come to New York

City instead. He remembered the first winter as having been extremely cold. And he didn't have a permanent place to stay."

Meanwhile, the wave of personalities from the worlds of musical comedy and literature had continued to wash up on Algonquin shores well after the demise of the Round Table.

Musical comedy writer Alan Jay Lerner composed some of "I Could Have Danced All Night" and other hit songs from *My Fair Lady* in all-night writing stints with Frederick Loewe at the Algonquin and at his townhouse. He met his *My Fair Lady* collaborator, Loewe, just down the street at The Lambs Club, when the club was on West 44th. Ever grateful to the club, he left it 5 percent of his royalties from *Brigadoon*. Richard Rogers and Oscar Hammerstein wrote the title song of *Oklahoma* in the presidential suite of the 396-room Omni-Berkshire Hotel, which opened in 1926.

The Rose and Oak room restaurants and famed lobby of the Algonquin have served as both playground and office to such legends in the theatre as drama critic/essayist George Jean Nathan, actress Julie Haydon (aka Mrs. George Jean Nathan) and Tennessee Williams' agent for many years, Audrey Wood, all of whom actually lived at the Royalton across the street.

Fast forward to the 1970's, the decade of the hotel's 75th birthday. This era really belonged to Andrew Anspach, Bodne's Yale-educated son-in-law, who through his love of the hotel, good living, celebrity and cabaret, returned the hotel to some of its former 1920's glamour and glory.

Demure, precise, genteel and an aficionado of people and tradition as well as of fine art and culture, Mr. Anspach may have run the place but he was also its most cultured guest. I had lunch with him many times and he was one of those rare people who made you feel like you were the center of the universe.

He had a way, like a good stage manager, of setting the scene so beautifully that you were, however briefly, the show's star attraction. Even though my father had lived at the hotel for a number of years and I had visited him there, I really didn't have the "feel" for the place other than a cursory knowledge of the Round Table and an appreciation of the hotel's lobby as a place to have a wonderful dessert. Until, that is, I ran into Mr. Anspach's infectious enthusiasm for the place. So when I wrote a 75th anniversary story about The Algonquin for *The Christian Science Monitor* in 1978 I had an understanding of the place that mere reading about it could never have afforded me.

I still asked myself then and over the years what a "literary type" hotel like The Algonquin had to do with *Christian Science Monitor* readers in Iowa or California? But as Ian Lloyd-Jones, president of Camberly Hotels, which ran the hotel for some years in the 1990's, said, the hotel has been inhabited by "not just celebrities but people who weave through the fabric of our lives." We were talking in his wood-paneled office in Atlanta where I had gone to see the opening of my play *If It Was Easy* at the Seven Stages Theatre. "Some of them are not quite as impressive as others. Louis Farakan this weekend. Billy Joel, Sting, has stayed there."

Like many hotel people, Mr. Lloyd-Jones really loves hotels, wherever they are. "I've lived in Atlanta for many, many years," he went on to regale me, "and I was having a glass of wine with my neighbors and I said to them, 'How long have you folks been married?' The gentleman answered, 'Fifty years. We got married in Lexington, Kentucky. And we spent our honeymoon night at The Brown hotel.' There are hundreds of registration cards from people who spent $4 back in 1945, 1946 and we tell them, 'If you send it in you can stay here for $4 today.' Just two weeks ago I'm at The Jefferson Hotel in Washington, D.C. and we're in the middle of a $3 million renovation upgrade and one of the workers has found an old rust-encrusted key to a guest room and he gave it to us and I'm in a meeting and I said to everybody at the meeting, 'Let's find out about this key. It will tell us something.' And I dropped it in a glass of Coca-Cola and four hours later we rubbed it clean and this key, which had been at The Jefferson Hotel for I don't know how long, said on it 'The Brown Hotel, Louisville, Kentucky, Room 805.' "

"What are you going to do to this lobby?" a nervous Andrew Anspach asked Ian Lloyd-Jones at this first meeting when Cambery took over management of The Algonquin. "Well, I was thinking about maybe some music, a string quartet," Mr. Jones replied. To which Mr. Anspach responded, "Our music is our conversation. Don't you hear it?" "What?" "The music! Conversation is our music."

"Steve Ross was the first entertainer I booked into the Oak room," cabaret impresario Donald Smith told me. "I had given Steve his London debut and California and he went off to do other things. I wasn't really able to handle another person and I was introduced to Michael Feinstein (Feinstein), who was searching for something and then that was very exciting. And then, of course, after Michael there was Andrea Marcovicci. But we put a lot of people there. I gave Julie Wilson a three or four month engagement there because the problem with cabaret is that you go to something you like and tell your friends and then the next night it's finished...I mean, Andrea, did eleven weeks there this year. Sold out."

In 1987, the Aoki Corporation of Japan purchased the Algonquin and poured $22 million into renovating the 165 rooms, public areas and behind-the-scenes mechanical and electrical work. In doing so Aoki saved the institution Edna Ferber called "a mother's knee" from the wrecking ball for at least another several decades.

Today, the Algonquin carries on the tradition of Case and Bodne and Anspach with its charm, linked to illustrious literary history and its world famous Oak Room cabaret. The Oak Room, where the Round Table once held court, attracts such performers as Karen Akers, Lillian Montevecci and Mary Clere Haran, who *The New Yorker* has hailed as "the most literate chanteuse of the current generation." Michael Feinstein, now an international star with a nightclub at the Regency Hotel—Feinstein's at the Regency—named after him, started out at The Algonquin's Oak Room in the mid-1980's.

Like artist Milton Glaser, cabaret superstar and Broadway actress Andrea Marcovicci, who was hailed by Stephen Holden of *The New York Times* as New York's "unofficial custodian" of old-time glamour, has a hard time choosing a favorite New York hotel. "This hotel and the St. Regis because I had my wedding at the St. Regis," Marcovicci told me after her show, "A Tribute to Fred Astaire," at the Algonquin's Oak Room in December 2004. "And because my daddy loved the St. Regis and we used to dance on the roof I have incredible memories of the St. Regis. I have very fond memories of the Sherry-Netherland Hotel because my father took me there as well." Marcovicci's father was a medial doctor who worked for the St. Regis and other hotels.

In October, 1912, The Algonquin was the scene of a late night escapade that was a cross between a madcap Keystone Kops silent serial and *Grand Hotel*. An intruder, a Paul Renaud, apparently broke into the suite occupied by playwright Eugene Walter (*Paid in Full*) and his actress wife, the beautiful Charlotte Walker. According to an article in the October 16, 1912 *Toledo Blade* newspaper, Mrs. Walter was still having storm-related "nightmares." When Walter heard his wife's first yell, he called in from his room, "Go to sleep; your bed isn't afloat," a reference to the great Galveston hurricane of 1910, which his wife experienced. Then, however, she yelled again. Walter wearing "only his pants pajamas," came to his wife's assistance. A great commotion erupted with Walter and the elevator operator and probably Charlotte Walker coming "right out into the hall in their nighties." Among the other theatrical guests at the hotel were actress Elsie Janis, actor Rex Beach and the famed John Drew, John Barrymore's uncle and Drew Barrymore's great uncle. Ethel Barrymore, John's sister, was staying there, also actor William Farnum. Another guest, tenth floor resident Colonel Bill Gag, who the article describes as a "globe trotter and mining expert," gave chase on the fire escape. The hotel had multiple non-connected fire escapes. The hotel manager, Frank Case, eventually nabbed Renaud on the eleventh floor. Interestingly, the charge the intruder was held on was for "questionable pictures" he happened to be carrying.

Charlotte Walker apparently wanted the intruder to get off with a "lecture," according to a subsequent article in the *New York American*. Renaud could not post bail set at $500. Renaud, who spoke French but no English, had "been arrested in practically every country in Europe," according to another contemporary account. Walker had not, however, thought he was going to be imprisoned when she attended his trial wearing a "velvet gown and heavy furs."

This was the same Eugene Walter who several years later in 1919 climbed up the fire escape of the then posh Alexandria Hotel in downtown Los Angeles, clambered into a suite, and allegedly punched his ex-girlfriend, former Ziegfeld Follies girl Nina Whitmore, in the face. Whitmore had been in a show in New York in 1911 called *The Merry Ronders* at the time Walter was enjoying some of his greatest success on Broadway, enjoying the hospitality of The Algonquin, and, apparently, enjoying the charms of Ms. Whitmore.

Singer/actress Wynne Miller, the niece of the late bandleader Glenn Miller, appeared at the Oak Room of the Algonquin Hotel in late February 2004 in her one-woman show "To Glenn with Love" to commemorate the Centenary of Miller's birth on March 1, 1904. In the admiring audience were novelist Tom Wolfe and nostalgia radio talk show host Joe Franklin.

"I remember seeing my uncle Glenn and my father up on the high school roof practicing at odd hours of the morning," Ms. Miller told me in an interview. "This was in Greeley, Colorado, before he became a household name here in New York in the late 1930's and in the Rouge Room of the Hotel Pennsylvania in 1940. Glenn came to the Hotel Pennsylvania in mid-1940. They weren't prepared for what was going to happen. Kids were driving 60, 70, 80 miles to see him!"

"I have heard Wynne before but this is the best I've ever heard," Mr. Wolfe, who was an avid fan of Glenn Miller's, told me. "She has such incredible range." Referring to the paucity of big band music around today, Mr. Wolfe smiled and said, "I noticed that there wasn't a whole lot of this sort of music at the Grammy's."

Mr. Wolfe, who has become identified as much for wearing his trademark white suit as his seemingly effortless prose and tales of New York, became a reporter on the old New York *Herald Tribune* in 1962 before publishing his first book, *The Kandy-Kolored Tangerine-Flake Streamline Baby*, in 1965.

Glenn Miller, who was born in Clarinda, Iowa, died during World War II when his plane was lost over the English Channel.

Wynne Miller played the part of Daisy Mae in the musical *Lil' Abner* and went on to become a cabaret singer of some note. "In the dear dead days of the past I was at the St. Regis Hotel at the Maisonette at the end of the great cabaret era," she told me.

"I knew Glenn before he was at the Hotel Pennsylvania," said Gary Stevens, a longtime New York syndicated columnist who knew and wrote about Miller. "My first impression of him was that this was a man who was on the brink of getting out of the band business months before because he couldn't meet his payroll when he was at the Paradise restaurant (on the second floor of the Brill Building). It was through the good wishes and bankroll of Tommy Dorsey who helped him get through and said, 'Listen, Glenn, you're ahead of your time. That sound you've got with this band is going to catch on. So stay with it!'" As a result, Miller was able to finish that engagement. Then he was booked through his agent, a very hard-driving salesman who headed GAC, Tom Rockwell, into the Glenn Island Casino and that's where it all happened. He came to the Hotel Pennsylvania in mid-1940. They weren't prepared for what was happening so quickly. "Glenn didn't put the Hotel Pennsylvania on the map," Mr. Stevens continued. "He certainly enhanced it. The Pennsylvania helped put him on the map." Miller had an eye for talent and he enjoyed taking people to the Astor Roof to see Tommy Dorsey. He told friends that, "You know, there's this kid that's singing with Tommy who's going to be big." That kid was Frank Sinatra.

Singer Maude Maggart, a protégé of Andrea Marchovicci, joined many others when she brought some of the glamour of the 1920's to the legendary Oak Room of the hotel in her show in early 2004. Like Marchovicci, she said the late Helen Morgan, who played Julie in the original production of *Showboat* in the 1920's, was an idol of hers. "Helen Morgan had a little voice and of course there were no microphones to use," Ms. Maggart said. "She would go into these speakeasies in the 1920's and quiet down a raucous audience with the power of what she had inside."

The fabulous and varied cultural history of the Algonquin makes it loom large on the New York hotel stage even though it may be overshadowed by other, newer hotels, in terms of décor and celebrity. After all, there's an awful lot of competition in New York, and no place more so than in the hotel business. John Jacob Aston IV, for one, made it his business that no hotel overshadowed his St. Regis, the tallest hotel in the world in 1905.

CHAPTER 4

THE ST. REGIS:
MR. ASTOR'S LITTLE INN

When John Jacob Astor IV sank down into the soothing warm water of his oversized tub with the gold-washed fixtures, he had reason to sigh and smile with self-satisfaction. Astor and his mother, Caroline Webster Schermerhorn Astor, had moved into their cavernous green mansard-roofed mansion on Fifth Avenue and 65th Street in 1895 after their old digs on Fifth Avenue and 34th Street had been intruded upon by cousin William Waldorf Astor's Waldorf Hotel on 33rd Street. John Jacob had become the new star of a star-strewn family by first constructing the more sumptuous Astoria "addition" to the original Waldorf in 1898, then, just five years later, opening the finest and tallest hotel in the world 21 blocks to the north.

The hotel was a masterstroke of understated elegance, a haven for the super-rich much the same as Claridge's in London. If the Plaza has many similarities to the Savoy in London—big, located next to the best that nature has to offer (the Thames for the Savoy and Central Park for the Plaza)—the St. Regis, which has a front entrance tucked away shyly on a side street, was more like a hidden jewel box.

Architects Trowbridge & Livingston patterned it after classic French designs of the period. Moreover, it set construction standards which, for the sheer amount of marble and other precious building materials, have, proportionately at any rate, yet to be exceeded. Mr. Astor spent $5.5 million on the hotel, which had marble floors and staircases, crystal chandeliers and Louis XV furniture. The library, containing 3,000 leather-bound books, had its own librarian. A primitive but surprisingly effective air-conditioning system and the city's first hotel mail chute were radical innovations of their day. Another novel feature was one of the city's first central vacuum systems. Maids plugged their vacuums into the wall and the powerful central vacuum would suck out carpet dust and refuse.

"For the third time in the history of the Astor family one of its members has had a hotel built, which is in its way different from and better than any other hotel then existing in the country," proclaimed the *Architectural Record* of June, 1904. "At the present time it is, with its eighteen stories, the highest hotel building open for business in New York City…It is intended for a class of people, both New Yorkers and transients, who want absolutely the best quality of hotel accommodations, and who do not mind paying for it …. By a happy combination of circumstances, the architects, Messrs. Trowbridge and Livingston; the owner, Colonel John Jacob Astor; the leasee, Mr. M. Haan and the contractors, under the general direction of Messrs. Marc Eidlitz & Son, were all united upon the same idea, and neither time, expense, care nor talent were spared in order to make the achievement satisfactory."

The New York Daily Tribune reported on September 4, 1904, that the St. Regis Hotel, "representing some $5,500,000 and several years work, was opened for a private view yesterday afternoon. This morning it will be ready for business…Designed to be the finest hotel in the world, and built under orders from Colonel [John Jacob] Astor to spare no expense, the St. Regis represents a high achievement. The architects, Messrs. Trowbridge & Livingston, have given almost their entire time to it for the last three years, while Mr. Haan [the leasee] has been planning and creating ideals for the last two decades."

Henry Holt and Company's *Rider's New York City*, a kind of Zagat Guide of its day, said twelve years after the St. Regis was built—and four years after Astor had himself gone down on the *Titanic*:

"The S.W. corner of 55th Street is occupied by the *Gotham Hotel*, a house especially admirable for guests remaining an extended period, and the S.E. by the *St. Regis Hotel*, a superlatively luxurious house, planned and run for the comfort of multi-millionaires. (Trowbridge & Livingston, architects). In the Palm Room is a fine mural The Story of Psyche, by *Robert V.V. Sewell*. Among its other decorations the hotel possesses several 17th Century Brussels tapestries, woven by *I. Van Zeunen*."

The Astors, by Harvey O'Connor (Alfred A. Knopf, 1941), claims that Vincent Astor (John Jacob Astor's son) may have "conceived of the world's problems in much the same light as those of his own St. Regis Hotel. In piping times he had sold it, but it bounced back during the

Great Depression. Graciously he installed Raymond Moley, the criminologist, brain-truster journalist, in charge as receiver and then summoned clever architects to make over his father's old building into the smartest hotel in New York. The St. Regis became the first wholly air-conditioned hotel in the world; its Iridium Room was the rendezvous of café society; its blue ice for bluebloods reflected the creative imagination of its owner, who saw red ink change into black."

Chase W. Parker in his 1931 *New York, The Wonder City*, applauded the 22-story addition to the St. Regis: "Within the past year a new addition has been added to the famous St. Regis as large as the main building itself, which has recently been altered and modernized, thus making the aristocratic old St. Regis one of the newest and most imposing of New York's magnificent hotels. John Jacob Astor built the original St. Regis, which at the time of completion was the grandest and most luxurious hotel in the world—the furniture was especially made in Paris. The new 'Seaglade' and Roof Garden restaurants are certainly superb, as is the main 'Oakroom' dining hall.

Ass'd. Val. $6,500,000
255 feet high .... 22 floors
650 guest rooms
Completed 1905 and 1929
Owner: Durham Realty Co.
Architect .... Sloan & Robertson
Builder .... Leddy & Moore"

In the beginning and throughout its nearly 100 year history, service at Mr. Astor's little inn was as paramount as the ornamentation.

"Anyone who wants to work here, they cannot be hired unless I give them the stamp of approval. I am looking for people that can smile, if they have a positive attitude." I was having breakfast with Gunther Richner, one of the foremost hoteliers, in the Astor Court of the St. Regis Hotel. This was during his second tour of duty at the St. Regis, having been the general manager of the Stanhope and the Drake, now known as the Swiss Hotel New York, in between.

Like an actor or talk show host, Mr. Richner has always wanted to please his "audience" ever since he first started working as a waiter in his native East Germany. Unlike an actor, his audiences are the guests in the house that Astor, John Jacob Astor IV, built in 1904.

"If they are in for the money or the short run…then I need to know if they have a problem with being a servant," he added. "If they have a problem with being a servant—and I gather that—I don't have to ask that. Then I would not hire them."

Europe and its grand hotels has a long tradition of service. Hotels, after all, were where the lords and ladies, the counts and countesses, used to stay when they came to London as they still do to some extent at the Ritz, or Claridge or Savoy Hotels. They didn't demand the utmost service; they expected it. But after William Waldorf Astor built his Waldorf Hotel at Fifth Avenue and 33rd Street, America finally had a proper hotel palace.

John Jacob Astor's son, Vincent, sold the hotel where bartender Fernard Petiot first introduced the Bloody Mary (it was originally called the "red snapper") in 1934, to the Duke tobacco family (actually Duke Management). The Dukes built an addition in 1927 but much like the Plaza's addition in 1921, it lacked the original building's opulence. Vincent Astor bought back the hotel in 1935 and three years later, as the waves of the Great Depression receded, he opened the Iridium Room (not to be confused with the current Iridium Room on Broadway), complete with an ice-skating rink, rolled out from the orchestra floor.

Jack Astor, John Jacob Astor's son, and Vincent's younger brother had survived the *Titanic* in his mother's womb, and was left a paltry several million dollars. Vincent, on the other hand, went on to inherit the vast sum of some $67 million.

Ivan Obolensky, the son of Vincent Astor's sister, Alice, told me that in Brooke Astor's apartment, Vincent was "relegated to a vitreen."

"Jack Astor was a half Astor," Mr. Obolensky began. "And he was in the 'bread basket' when the *Titanic* went down. He was a very nice, strange man. Very nice to me. And wanted me to sue Brooke when she got all that money. I said, 'I can't do that.' He did sue. He got, I think, $250,000…He bought Fox Hollow Farm in Rhinebeck. He went all over Europe buying twelve of the greatest bulls and twelve of the greatest heifers and turned them all loose in the field. It was a debacle."

"I had the temerity as a young man to go to Vincent and say, 'Uncle Vincent, I've got a proposition for you. You've got the St. Regis free and clear. We have the Ambassador, which has a fair amount of debt. And you have Astor Plaza that you are trying to get financed. We'll go and pool our three resources and when you build Astor Plaza…put all debt of the three entities on Astor Plaza…And the way we would do this is we would put so many floors aside for business and we would run special elevators for that side of it and it would be set up with as many floors as it would take to rent for business to cover the nut for the entire three entities…He was so furious that I had the temerity to come to him about it—because he didn't really do very much with his business—he made mistakes—sold out too soon on something. (One of these was Poverty Row, which is now opposite Gracie Mansion.) That's when the Astor office was on 85th Street. 1 East 85th Street. That was where the office was when my father began in his real estate…He literally dispossessed me from that point on. That's why I lost $200 million…Brooke came in and Vinnie was all for me and Brooke came in just at the wrong time and that's the end of it.

Mr. Obolensky, it turns out, is a pretty good source for all sorts of family and hotel world lore: "The Obolenskys apparently have a huge mystique; they were liberal and my father was put in jail [in Russia] because he wanted to have a liberal government at all costs.

"The Ambassador Hotel was a total and absolute bonanza when it was sold for $4 million…I think we had $600,000 sunk in all told…We got the cream of the cream because of all those non-taxable situations, and my father for the first time made money ….

"I remember when the St. Regis was knee-deep at the bar. And women would come in looking for their husbands or whatever—and the husbands would beat a hasty retreat out the other two exits. They weren't trapped like rats (with their girlfriends)."

Smaller than either The Plaza or The Waldorf-Astoria, the St. Regis attracted many famous guests who liked living there better than at either of the two other bigger hotels.

Perhaps the most famous person to have ever stayed at the St. Regis, was Salvadore Dali.

"Whenever Dali was in New York and through the War and afterwards he took refuge in the St. Regis where he set himself up in the extremely lucrative business of painting the portraits of society ladies," Meryle Secrest writes in her biography of the great modern artist. "He was, of course, capable on occasion of parodying his subjects but he did it with such a deft brush—as in the case of art collector Chester Dale (who lived with some of his collection at The Plaza), depicted showing a solemn and unmistakable resemblance to his poodle—that one gathers the barb went unnoticed." But according to the author, Ann Woodward refused to pay the asked price (maybe as high as $25,000) because she felt the portrait of her husband

William Woodward was not suitable. Marie-Therese Nichols, the wife of William I. Nichols, once a prominent editor, also had her portrait done. When Dali later found out it had been given away he was furious. "Somebody so stupid as to give away a Dali has to be a cuckold!" he exclaimed.

"Dining at the St. Regis when Dali was dining was always a lively affair," Secrest recounts. "He took his dinner partners by the hand or arm when he talked, loudly and energetically."

If there is something in the walls, rooms, bones of the Hotel Chelsea that inspires, the same is true for the St. Regis. Salvadore Dali, for example, had his studio on the hotel's second floor, where models would pose for hours on end. When he gave a party it was sometimes an affair of international intrigue.

Dali occupied a cavernous suite on an upper floor of the hotel but had made a deal with the management to pay exactly half of what he consumed, according to Dali friend Martin Riskin, one of the hotel's former top executives. Half his hotel suite costs, half his food bills, half his liquor bills and half his party bills. The hotel got plenty of publicity in the process—and narrowly escaped getting plenty of unwanted publicity.

These are some St. Regis secrets I've uncovered:

When one of Dali's two pet ocelots destroyed a $30,000 Persian rug in Dali's suite the hotel manager asked the great artist, per their agreement to pay exactly half—or $15,000—for a replacement. Red-faced, Dali walked out of the meeting, saying "Dali will not pay one penny!" Well, every month he was dunned for the carpet and every month he refused to pay until one day a friend of Dali's who worked at the hotel saw a painting of Dali's heading up to the manager's office and his debt was never spoken of again!

On another occasion, Dali held an elaborate party in the St. Regis wine cellar and at midnight, the banquet manager, seeing everything was under control, went home feeling that it was a job well done. Well, at 2 a.m., when he got a call from his assistant, he knew something was up. His assistant was almost in hysterics.

"One of Dali's models is walking up and down the big table in the wine cellar and the guests including Mr. Dali are throwing glasses of wine on her," the assistant blurted out almost in tears. "Oh, my God!" the banquet manager responded. "Her dress will be ruined!" "What dress!? She's naked!" "I'll be right there," the manager responded, not wanting the incident to "make the papers!"

Dali, who craved publicity and the limelight, actually chose to live at The St. Regis, because he could have more privacy there than at The Plaza or a bigger hotel. In his studio on the second floor he'd be hard at work for hours sketching beautiful models. Only when the hotel would bring him some refreshment would the strokes on his canvas pause. "Get out of there with your whores!" his wife sometimes banged on the door of the studio.

"Please, madam, the master is working," the discreet hotel staff was instructed to say.

Martin Riskin was director of banquets at the St. Regis when Salvadore Dali's longtime friendship with Baron Philippe de Rothschild was sorely tested.

"Baron Philippe de Rothschild greatly enjoyed visiting New York, feeling very comfortable in an elegant suite at the Pierre Hotel. He especially found pleasure by entertaining friends at the Pierre, sharing his pride and joy Chateau Mouton-Rothschild with them," Mr. Riskin told me.

"When World War II ended the Baron reclaimed his vineyard and originated the brilliant idea of each year commissioning a leading contemporary artist to design the top of the Mouton-Rothschild label. For the 1958 vintage Baron Philippe selected his friend Salvadore Dali who painted a daliesque lamb, as Dali told me some years later: "A 'mouton' for Mouton."

"After Dali's beautiful book in honor of his wife *The Dinners of Gala*" was printed, I suggested to Dali a companion book which would be entitled *The Wines of Gala*." Riskind continued. "Dali liked the concept and asked me to write the introduction, which I did, in English. When Baron Philippe heard about the new book he wrote a long mystical poem in French which Dali decided to use as the introduction. To celebrate the wine book's publication, Baron Philippe came to New York, staying at the Pierre as usual. Every year Dali lived at the St. Regis hotel for a few months, greatly enjoying the stir he caused in New York especially when he went walking on Fifth Avenue accompanied by his two pet ocelots.

"During the years I served as the Director of Banquets at the St. Regis, when Dali was there I would encounter him virtually every day and we became quite friendly. However, now I had a problem. The difficulty consisted of logistics. Baron Philippe wanted Dali to come to his suite at The Pierre, while Dali wanted the Baron to come to his suite at The St. Regis. I needed to find a solution involving two very special people, both of whom I was friendly with, and did not wish to alienate. When they remained adamant for a couple of days I proposed a situation which I hoped would please both.

"In the St. Regis we had a charming small wine cellar where our finest wines were kept. By removing all of the wines with the exception of Chateau Mouton Rothschild we would create a miniature Rothschild wine cellar in the St. Regis. The Baron and Dali accepted the idea and when the cordial meeting took place both felt their pride had been preserved."

Dali came to private dinner parties, large and small, at The Carlyle but his New York home always remained the St. Regis, which went to great length to serve him, his whims, his ocelots and his wife.

Gunther Richter was first a general manager of the St. Regis in the late 1970's after working at The Waldorf-Astoria from 1974 to 1978. He then moved back to the St. Regis nearly a quarter century later. "I was at the St. Regis when Salvadore Dali was here for the last time, I believe, in 1979. Fred Astaire was here at that time, too. Salvador Dali came with a reptile...He had a suite and another room for the reptile. Because the reptile has to be in the bathtub."

Mr. Richter actually lived at the Americana, now the Sheraton Center, while the old Hotel Taft was being renovated to become the Grand Bay Hotel. "They got me the manager's apartment of the Sheraton because the owners of our company were affiliated with the Sheraton. And at that time in 1986 the Grand Bay became the best hotel on the West side. The owners of the hotel were the Equitable Life Insurance and the chairman of the company had a soft heart for hardware and he made sure that the quality of marble and woodwork and art was high."

Many other entertainers, authors and celebrities stayed and sang at the St. Regis. The late jazz great Mabel Mercer, a supreme stylist who influenced Frank Sinatra and other household name singers, sang at the St. Regis.

Michael Arlen, who wrote the novel *The Green Hat*, was one of the hotel's celebrity guests. After Arlen's dramatization of his novel he cabled Broadway producer Al Woods that he would accept his offer of an option fee. "And then the Armenian novelist-dramatist, born Dikran Koujoumdjan in Roustchouk, Bulgaria, decided to make his first crossing of the Atlantic and have a look at those astonishing Americans," my father wrote in his book *Matinee Tomorrow*. "On his first day in New York, Woods called upon him at the Ritz-Carlton and presented him with a case of whiskey; on the second day Woods sent over a welcome-to-New York gift, a platinum wristwatch encircled with diamonds. "I'm going to like America," Arlen said. "I'm going to like it very much."

Like many of New York's legendary hotels, the St. Regis has undergone many a facelift through the years. Much of the credit for the most recent gutting and redoing of the St. Regis belongs to John Kapoltas, ITT CEO, the parent company of Starwood Hotels, who insisted the St. Regis be returned to its former glory and become the flagship of the company. It also became the centerpiece of the chains' architectural gems, which include the Jefferson Hotel in Richmond, Virginia, the Carleton in Washington, D.C. and the Palace in San Francisco. They and others form what is now called the St. Regis group of hotels. Starwood Hotels has renamed its top-of-the-line properties St. Regis brand hotels, including the St. Regis Grand in Rome and the top floors of the Essex House, now called the St. Regis Club.

"We're hoping to do a big gala on the St. Regis Roof which will mark a major anniversary of Mabel's (Mercer) passing," Donald Smith, who runs the New York Cabaret Convention told me, "It's very hard to believe: Julie Wilson's 90th birthday and the 15th anniversary of the Cabaret convention. So I'm thinking, it started at the St. Regis in 1985 with a dinner dance.

"When Mabel first came here from England, it was to sing at Rueben Blue, on 52nd Street between 5th and 6th Avenues. At the time, Paula Lawrence was headlining at Reuben Blue. Mabel was there six years and when she left there she went to a place called the By-line Room...Sylvia Sims and Portia Nelson and Barbara Carol were downstairs and they'd come to listen to Mabel."

Opening in 1991, Lespinasse was named for Mademoiselle de Lespinasse, who had a Paris salon where the topics of the day were discussed. It closed in early 2003, felled by the economic slowdown and lingering effects of the 2001 terrorist attacks on the World Trade Center which knocked the wind out of international tourism.

Like Bible kings, The Plaza, St. Regis, Pierre, Carlyle, and Waldorf-Astoria share some of the city's most unusual hospitality history. After all, it was at the St. Regis that those who built The Plaza discussed and refined their game plan.

Across Fifth Avenue from The St. Regis was the Gotham, which is now the Peninsula. Hotelier and developer Evelyn Sharp, whose son, Peter, ran The Carlyle, lived in the Penthouse of the Gotham with a huge private art collection, including Chagalls, Miros and Picassos. "It was here that she made her deals, in one year buying three hotels," Marie Brenner wrote in a *New York* magazine article.

The St. Regis was sold by the Nacional Hostelera (Balsa Hotels) which had operated the hotel since 1960, in 1965 to Wellington Associates. "This will be a forever hotel—and a famous one," Sol Goldman of Wellington promised, to quiet fears that the company had plans to raze the remarkable property.

The St. Regis, like all hotels, has had some less than elegant moments as well.

"When I worked on *Valley of the Dolls* at Fox in 1967 in New York City I met writer Jacqueline Susanne, who showed up for an interview with a reporter from the *New York Post* at the St. Regis restaurant," Charles Barrett, the movie and TV publicist, told me. "She ordered a 'California' tossed salad and then complained to the waiter that she saw a bug crawling in it. The reporter (cannot recall his name) was quite amused and wrote about it too. I was there with my boss, the late Jay Remer of 20th Fox...I was just a PR person in training then. The St. Regis gave us all free lunch because we had a party there that evening for the movie."

"When I was at the St. Regis the general manager was Charles Harry, who was a knight of Malta," Martin Riskin said. "He retired and went to the Vatican and became a priest." The resident manager was Frank Burmingham. He became a manager at The Waldorf and was at the Riga Royal for some years.

John Jacob Astor followed the tradition of very wealthy men dying heroically. Alfred Gwynn Vanderbilt, for instance, who perished when the *Lusitania* was struck by a German U-boat torpedo, instructed his manservant to gather as many children as he could into lifeboats. "Jack Astor died a hero," Karl Schriftgiesser wrote in his book *Oscar of the Waldorf.* "While the band played 'Nearer My God to Thee' aboard the stricken ship (the *Titanic*) he lifted his wife, then five months pregnant, into a boat and asked to accompany her. The officer replied that no men might get in until all the women were accommodated...Astor then waved good-bye to Madelaine and turned to busy himself with helping fill another boat.

"He left behind a tremendous fortune: $63,000,000 in real estate and $24,000,000 in personal property. Of that $10,400,000 represented his holdings in the Astoria Hotel (the addition of the Waldorf, which opened in 1897). His holdings in the St. Regis Hotel were appraised at the time at $3,975,000."

Astor's death, followed by Vanderbilt's death, marked the end of the gilded era and the beginning in a splurge of building residential hotels and then, in the early 1930's, newer grander palaces than the first Waldorf-Astoria.

Today, for example, it's not uncommon to see titled nobility sit before a roaring fire at The Savoy and unwrap their Christmas presents at Christmastime. And after William Waldorf Astor, American royalty if there was any, built The Waldorf, they had their proper palace at last. When The St. Regis opened it was a kind of palace, compared to the rambling Waldorf-Astoria.

The St. Regis helped make already posh Fifth Avenue even posher. The Beaux-Arts Gotham Hotel opened the following year at a cost of $2.25 million (considerably less than the St. Regis, it should be noted). Its elaborate limestone carvings and Doric columns were designed to compliment the University Club across the street. The Gotham remained a residential apartment hotel until 1978. Designer Pierre Cardin then renovated it in 1987 when it reopened as Maxim's de Paris. Hong Kong and Shanghai Hotels, Limited, reopened it in 1988 as the U.S. flagship of the Peninsula Group.

But even as the splendid St. Regis was first opening its ornate doors to the rich and fabulous, a far different kind of hotel was popping up directly to the west and slightly to the south in a far different region of the city, Longacre Square—soon to be redubbed Times Square.

CHAPTER 5

NAUGHTY, BAWDY TIMES SQUARE HOTELS AND BROADWAY

Times Square's Astor hotel was the playground for Broadway show people. "It was still up in the 1940's," Paula Lawrence told me in speaking about the Astor Hotel, on Broadway and 44th Street. "Also, when I was very little it was a very desirable place. When I was about five or six I had an operation and when I got better, they didn't want to take me home. I had a brother and sister who had the chicken pox. So my father said, 'Where would you like to stay—we'll take you to a hotel.' I chose the Astor because it was on Broadway and I wanted to see all the Broadway lights. It was very grand in those days. It had a huge ballroom. And it was a great place to give opening night parties. I remember the opening night party for *Winged Victory* was there because it had such a huge cast."

Did she know the roof garden during Prohibition? "I don't go back *that* far," Ms. Lawrence said.

"The Astor Hotel was very glamorous," said the late syndicated columnist Gary Stevens. "In fact, Toscanini lived in the Astor Hotel. And he used to come up every other night to listen to Tommy Dorsey. He loved Tommy. He loved the sound of his trombone. He had a table near the window and he'd close his eyes when he wasn't having his dinner and just listen to Tommy. The publicity man for the hotel, Hy Gardner, who later became a columnist for the *Herald Tribune*, had a great sense of humor and went to Toscanini one night and said, 'Maestro, I see you're coming up three or four times a week,' and Toscanini said, 'Oh, I love Tommy and his trombone. It makes me feel good to hear that sound.' And Hy said, 'Just don't get any ideas to steal him for the NBC Symphony because we've got him signed for the next year!'"

45

"Meet me at the Astor" was part of the social vocabulary of the 1920s before and after the Great Depression, which helped curb the number of Broadway openings from nearly 300 in 1927 to around 100 in the early 1930s. Even in the 1950s the hotel was going great guns but the 1960s, as the Vietnam War raged, took its toll on the Astor which began to show signs of the same urban decay as its less celebrated neighbors.

The stubborn final steel girder, which had once been at the crossroads of the so called "golden age" of Broadway in the 1920s and later, was razed on February 23, 1968.

Max Rosoff, who first opened a restaurant across from the old Hippodrome on Sixth Avenue near 44th Street, moved to the first floor of the old Metropol Hotel on 43rd Street, just east of Broadway in 1919, the year my father first set foot in Manhattan and Times Square. Max named his new restaurant Rosoff's, which also became the name of the hotel. It's now known as The Copacabana on 43rd Street. Rosoff's (the restaurant) quickly became a favorite of the Broadway crowd and counted among its patrons over the years Shakespearean actor Walter Hampden, Rex Harrison, Rosalind Russell (she of *His Girl Friday* fame, opposite Cary Grant, which was a remake of *The Front Page*, written by a couple of hard-bitten old Times Square newspapermen, Ben Hecht and Charles MacArthur) and Lee Tracy, who starred in my father's 1928 New York newspaper comedy-drama, *Gentlemen of the Press*. Rosoff's was the scene of a roaring blaze that had started in a defective flue and eventually attracted a gaping crowd of several thousand people from the Times Square area. If only they could have put it on a stage, they'd have had a smash hit. According to one news account, "the firemen got unexpected help from a group of their comrades who were attending a Uniformed Firemen's Association reception at the Claridge Hotel on Broadway and 44th Street." Some 75 guests who were staying on the 43rd Street side of the hotel were not disturbed.

Several years earlier, a retired waiter named Sidney Rose, who'd lived at the hotel for some 30 years, committed suicide in his fourth floor room at Rosoff's. It wasn't poverty that drove him to it. He left $6,150 in cash in a cigar box and some $26,000 in various bank accounts.

Hotels and theater people have been forever linked in New York and elsewhere in the United States and no more so than in Times Square. Stars like Enrico Caruso and Will Rogers stayed in the area's more lavish properties like The Knickerbocker and Astor Hotels while bit players stuck to the smaller hotels on the side streets. Two of the exceptions were—and still are—The Algonquin and the Royalton. John Barrymore and playwright Eugene Walter enjoyed the hospitality, convenience and quieter off-the-beaten-Broadway track quality of The Algonquin. My father, Ward Morehouse, lived there on and off and at one time kept two raccoons in his suite until the management ordered them out. The enterprising Morehouse quickly found a new home for them on the roof of the West 44th Street Hotel.

Long before this, in the early 1890s, Herald Square was the center of the theater world. Minnie Madden Fiske made her acting debut at the Standard Theatre. They wrote some of the songs and made the deals in hotels, which helped business in the theaters and the hotels.

The Park Avenue Hotel, built in 1886 was several blocks to the East of Herald Square. It, too, became a magnet for Herald Square stars but it's "absolutely fire proof" building, as it was advertised, was engulfed by a devastating fire nonetheless. Seventeen people died in the $3 million hotel that had been built around an inner courtyard and was known for its concerts.

The union of hospitality with the theater reached its zenith 112 years ago in 1893 when William Waldorf Astor's Waldorf Hotel first opened at Fifth Avenue and 33rd Street. Enter George C. Boldt, who was that man, legend has it, who either coined or employed the phrase "the customer is always right." Either way he certainly strove to give all his customers star treatment, making them feel they were the biggest stars on the city's brightest stage.

Seven years earlier in October, 1886, the Holland House helped change the course of theatrical history. A.C. Erlanger, Marc Klaw, Al Hayman, Samuel F. Nirdlinger, J. Frederick Zimmerman and the hyperactive Charles Frohman (who went down on the *Titanic* 16 years later) formed the notorious Syndicate. Over filet mignon and poached lobster these mighty producers and investors agreed to standardize cross-country bookings, making it possible for systematic tours through a central agency. (And cutting down on the control that some well-known players had over their careers.) Joseph Jefferson, best known for his theatrical rendition of Washington Irving's "Rip Van Winkle," and others railed against the Syndicate's iron-fisted control of venues and players. But Mrs. Fiske, who openly defied the Syndicate, often ended up playing in lodge halls—and even skating rinks.

A *Times* article from March, 1889, describes the transformation of the Rossmore Hotel into The Hotel Metropole. The "new" hotel, on Broadway just south of 42nd Street, had its debut on April 27, 1889. The *Times* writer was very impressed by its extensive renovations and explains the use of the color bronze in some areas, whereas other areas also had gold. As the Rossmore, it had advertised it was "3 blocks from Grand Central Depot."

There was a large, mixed sex dining hall which apparently covered an entire block between Broadway and Seventh Avenue. The building also featured a men-only café.

Playwright Eugene O'Neill was born in a hotel called the Barrett House, built in 1893, at 43rd Street and Broadway at a time when the West Forties were quieter and much more residential than the more ruckus Union and Herald Squares. In the eight-story Barrett House, the O'Neills "looked out on cobblestone streets, where horse-driven carriages passed at a leisurely pace," write Arthur and Barbara Gelb in *O'Neill*, their biography of the great dramatist. "The Barrett House set into a gabled tower, was a landmark for uptown residents and visitors."

"For many years O'Neill was to point out to friends the third-floor room until, in 1940, the hotel was torn down to make room for a two-story structure housing a group of stores and topped by a towering electric sign advertising Kleenex," the Gelbs continue. "'Every time I go past, I look up,' O'Neill said in 1925. 'Third window from Broadway on the Forty-Third Street side. I can remember my father pointing it out to me.'"

Of course, O'Neill lived in many palatial places in the intervening years between these two hotels, including a home that Carlotta, his third wife, helped design in Sea Island, Georgia, one of the so-called "golden isles," south of Savannah and north of Jacksonville, Florida. It was partly in the shape of a sailing ship, the kind of vessel O'Neill had sailed on himself as a young man seeking Jack London-like adventures.

Perhaps F. Scott Fitzgerald best captured the glamour and rhythm and rush of Times Square in the 1920s in the *Beautiful and the Damned*:

"The soft rush of taxis by him, and laughter, laughter hoarse as a crow's, incessant and loud, with the rattle of the subways underneath—and over all, the revolutions of light, the growings and recedings of light—light dividing like pearls—forming and reforming in glittering bars and circles and monstrous grotesque figures cut amazingly on the sky."

The pre-Times Square era of the west 40's, which included a motley array of horse stables and small manufacturers as well as hotels began to change almost overnight as theaters like the Hudson and New Amsterdam sprang up. But it was the Italian Renaissance Terra-cotta-clad 25-story New York Times Building, which opened with considerable fanfare on December 31, 1904, that made Times Square the city's first cultural center. As Marc Eliot writes in his book *Down 42nd Street*, "The opening of the IRT stop at 42nd Street between Broadway and Seventh Avenue coincided with *The New York Times* breaking ground on construction of its highly anticipated skyscraper headquarters. The two events combined to reconfigure Manhattan's midtown boulevard into a crossroads of recreation and commerce the likes of which had never been seen before in America. High-ticket entertainment, fabulous restaurants, luxury hotels such as the Knickerbocker, which both opera great Enrico Caruso and reigning theatrical 'superstar' of his day James O'Neill called their New York City home, modern underground transportation, and the newest northern border of the notorious Tenderloin with its well-equipped houses of prostitution—all shared space on the streets that immediately surrounded the *Times*'s new headquarters."

Caruso once occupied half a floor or 14 rooms at the Knickerbocker on Broadway and 42nd Street and regularly waved to his diehard fans. He loved the Knickerbocker's proximity to the Metropolitan Opera House, three blocks to the South. The building that had once been called "The 42nd Street Country Club" was on the doorstep of one of the city's greatest cultural institutions, and in the midst of old Broadway. He could at times be as bawdy as Broadway but enjoyed sketching friends, admirers and acquaintances. He once relieved himself from his bedroom window to the perverse delight of the crowd below. One of the couples he liked to sketch was the Cranes.

Harold Osband Crane and his wife Elizabeth were well-healed Chicagoans. Harold was the only surviving son of the wealthy Chicago Plate and Terne industrialist, Benjamin P. Crane and his wife Sarah Walter Crane. Elizabeth was related to the well known Chicago judge Thomas Taylor. Besides being an engineer, Harold Crane inherited the proceeds from his father's business interests. Caruso purportedly gave Harold and Elizabeth a portrait of themselves by his own hand. The Crane's later moved to and passed away in Carmel by the Sea, California, a well known artist colony. Their son Clarkson Crane (who also knew Caruso) was a well known author who would often relate this story to friends.

Caruso surprised many of his friends when in August of 1918 he married Miss Dorothy Park Benjamin, the daughter of a prominent patent attorney, at the Marble Collegiate Church at 29th Street and Fifth Avenue. In December of the following year, when Caruso was 46, Mrs. Caruso gave birth to a daughter they named Gloria.

The $3.3 million hotel was actually designed in 1901 but remained unfinished until Mr. Astor, who also owned the land under the hotel, agreed to complete it in 1905 after some of its original investors pulled out. Astor actually leased the southeast corner of 42nd Street to J.E. and A.C. Pennock, who hired Bruce Price and Marvin & Davis. One factor giving the investors cold feet was the hotel's "uptown" location. After all, the Knickerbocker wasn't known as "the Fifth Avenue Country Club" for no reason. But at the time it was pushing the boundaries of theatrical entertainment. Astor got the architectural firm of Trowbridge & Livingston to redesign the interior and it quickly became the place to be and be seen.

The Knickerbocker "had its own subway entrance (the door is still visible at the east end of the platform for Track 1 of the shuttle), pneumatic tubes to each sleeping floor for messages and, instead of the usual palm room, a flower room with live and cut flowers," Christopher Gray reported in *The New York Times*. With a gold dinner service for 48 and 500 Paris-made clocks (and an employee dedicated to winding them), the Knickerbocker was advertised as "a Fifth Avenue hotel at Broadway prices." What architectural writers noted most were the decorations of the restaurants, grill and bar. In other hotels the reproductions were typically of old masters, but The Knickerbocker had contemporary art. These included Frederic Remington, Frederick MacManie, James Wall Finn and, in the bar, Maxfield Parrish's painting of "Old King Cole," 8 feet wide by 30 feet long, which is now at the St. Regis.

The Real Estate Record and Guide predicted that the mural "will do what few works of art have ever done—it will pay its own way!"

A hundred years ago, the Times Square area really was the sort of "wild west" hotel capital of the city, with the more genteel establishments east of Fifth Avenue or on it. The building once occupied by the Hotel Knickerbocker is still standing. It actually closed as a hotel in 1919 with the advent of Prohibition and became an office building that once housed *Newsweek* magazine. Many of the offices in it have individual bathrooms— making them very desirable. The Astor was two blocks due north at 44th Street and Broadway. Further east, the Mansfield, which still exists. It was next to Sherry's Restaurant on Fifth Avenue. Further downtown, the Waldorf-Astoria with its Astoria addition even more grandiose and gilded than the original Waldorf, was in full flower. The Waldorf had been built in 1893 with its Astoria addition finished in 1897. Maude Adams, the first Peter Pan, loved to have tea there. As did George M. Cohan and Diamond Jim Brady. But in 1907, its biggest competition was the new Plaza Hotel. From the top-most suite in the Plaza you could see the ships, including some of the Cunard liners, in port on the Hudson.

The first decade of the 20th century was also an era in which hotel proprietors entertained almost as lavishly as those tireless builders of the grandest hotels, The Astors and Vanderbilts. While Alfred Guinn Vanderbilt threw a farewell dinner-dance in a ballroom suite of Sherry's on Fifth Avenue in February 1909, later that year James B. Regan, the proprietor of the Knickerbocker, entertained 60 of his New York hotel executive friends in the hotel's grand ballroom at a "sunken garden" Roman feast, complete with real sod and gravel walks. Even on the day it was announced the hotel was closing, May 30, 1919, Mr. Regan gave a lavish dinner party.

Little did I know when I lived at the old Lambs Club on West 44th Street, that almost directly outside my room, which faced south, was the infamous Hotel Metropole on 43rd Street just east of Broadway, which had become Rossoff's and is now the Casablanca. This isn't to be confused with another Hotel Metropole which stood at 42nd Street and Broadway. At the former Metropole (on 43rd Street), gangster Rosy Rosenthal was murdered on July 15, 1912, in one of the first drive-by gangland shootings. He'd been in the dining room several hours and when he stepped out into 43rd Street he was shot in a hail of bullets. The alleged assailant was Charles Becker, a lieutenant in the New York City Police Department. Other alleged conspirators were Dago Frank, Left Louie, Gyp the Blood and Whitey Lewis. But many said Becker was framed for the crime by gamblers trying to save their own lives. In any event, Becker is the one who took the rap, as reported at the time: "Charles Becker, a lieutenant on the New York City police force, was put to death in the electric chair in Sing Sing prison on July 30, 1915. He had been convicted…of murdering Herman Rosenthal, a gambler, who was shot and killed…on the morning of July 16, 1912."

F. Scott Fitzgerald in his 1925 novel *The Great Gatsby* immortalized the legend of Rosy Rosenthal. Here the character Wolfshiem, tells how Rosy was killed:

> "The old Metropole. The old Metropole. Filled with faces dead and gone. Filled with friends gone now forever. I can't

forget so long as I live the night they shot Rosy Rosenthal there. It was six of us at the table, and Rosy had ate and drunk a lot all evening. When it was almost morning the waiter came up to him with a funny look and says somebody wants to speak to him outside. 'All right,' says Rosy, and begins to get up, and I pulled him down in his chair.

"'Let the bastards come in here if they want you, Rosy, but don't you, so help me, move outside this room.' It was four o'clock in the morning then, and if we'd raised the blinds we'd of seen daylight."

Many Metropole furnishings sadly were destroyed or lost, like those of the old Biltmore Hotel years later (although some of the Biltmore's furnishings wound up in the Biltmore Room restaurant in the Chelsea section of Manhattan). Some, however, managed to wind up in unusual places. For example, a grand crystal chandelier from the old Waldorf-Astoria is reputed to be in the lobby of the Stanley Theatre in Jersey City, NJ, according to volunteer historians connected with the theater. While the grand four-sided clock graces the main lobby of the current Waldorf-Astoria.

In 1910, Broadway's theatrical life was centered in the Thirties but gradually the Rialto had been creeping ever northward. Lee and J.J. Shubert plunked down their offices at Broadway and 39th Street, opposite the Casino Theater, and they also had visions of a playhouse to the north of 42nd—at the corner of 50th on the site occupied by the American Horse Exchange. The Exchange had been extremely popular with New York society and was the property of William K. Vanderbilt.

Beyond 50th, northward by thirteen blocks at 63rd and Central Park West, popped up the New Theater, endowed by millionaires (and doomed to failure). As the New Theater began its second season with a brilliant premiere, William Vanderbilt occupied a box. Lee Shubert, serving as executive general manager, entered the Vanderbilt box and during an exchange of greetings the property at Broadway and 50th Street is mentioned. Yes, averred the illustrious millionaire, he might lease or sell, but wouldn't that be too far from the heart of Broadway for a strictly commercial playhouse? Lee Shubert didn't think so. He and his brother felt that there would be a great boom in theater building in the Forties and Fifties in another ten years.

The deal went through. The property at 1634 Broadway was leased by the brothers from Syracuse and it's a realty transaction that caused a stir in theatrical circles. It brought scornful laughter and comment from competitors. Marcus Loew chuckled to himself; so did Abe Erlanger, and E.F. Albee. "Broadway and 50th?" Why, that's out on the desert," ran the comment. "People won't go way up there to see a show. They'd be scared; there's not a light between the Hotel Astor and Columbus Circle." Upon this site, however, the enterprising and far-sighted Shuberts began the building of a playhouse to be called the Winter Garden, which opened in late March of 1911.

Broadway, as of 1911, had become New York's and America's Great White Way. Broadway sputtered with theater marquee displays, spelling out in blazing incandescence (the era of the neons and flea-circused 42nd Street was still years away) the names of the stars of the current hits…William Gillette in *Secret Service* at the Empire, Frances Starr in *The Easiest Way* at the Garrick, Maude Adams in *Chanticler* at the Knickerbocker, *Every Woman* at the Herald Square. Also, Christie MacDonald in *The Spring Maid*, Mrs. Fiske in *Becky Sharp*, Hazel Dawn in *The Pink Lady*, Holbrook Blinn in *The Boss*…. And then, for even more spectacular effect, there were the gigantic non-theatrical electric signs…"RUPPERT'S the Beer That Satisfies"…"Schaefer—Lager Beer"…the Black and White Scotch whisky sign on the roof of the building adjoining the Empire Theater…The Budweiser sign, Kelly-Springfield, Fisk Tires, Fatima cigarettes, Bull Durham, Robert Burns. Add to these the flashy signs from the famous restaurants and bars of the day— the Astor, Jack's, Delmonico's, Shanley's, the Claridge, Mee Chow Low, Reisenweber (way up at the Circle), and the inevitable Rector's.

Such, indeed, was the pre-war Great White Way, the Broadway of a comparative age of innocence, the Broadway that still hummed the "Merry Widow Waltz" and that was under the spell of "Alexander's Ragtime Band," as the Messrs. Shuberts, boldly, and as pioneers in an uncharted terrain, opened the Winter Garden with *La Belle Paree*, five blocks north of the Astor. The premiere was a spectacular event. Many distinguished persons attended. President Taft, one of the most theater-minded of the Chief Executives, doesn't make it, but all New York turns out. First-nighters come by motor, by foot, by trolley, by carriage. They come ermine-wrapped, and in sable; in mink and—here and there—in harem skirts. And in everything. W.K. Vanderbilt is impressively present. So, too, are dramatic critics of the time—Alan Dale, Acton Davies, Louis De Foe, Charles Darnton, and so on. The hit of the show is made by an unknown black-face comedian named Al Jolson, who, in the role of Erastus Sparkler, sings "Paris Is a Paradise for

Coons." The first-night intermission chatter is of the beauty of the new playhouse, of the mistake the Shuberts have made in building it so far up-town, and of the singer Jolson. The reviewers the next day predict that Jolson, once of Lew Dockstater's minstrels, and hired for the Winter Garden at $150 weekly, might some day make a name for himself.

La Belle Paree wasn't a success but the Shuberts, with great pride in their new theater and with many plans for it, installed the famous Winter Garden "runway" and had numerous additional productions: *Vera Violetta*, *The Passing Show of 1912* and *The Honeymoon Express*. The celebrated French star, Gaby Deslys, was brought over for *Vera Violetta* at the un-precedented salary of $5,000 a week. "Five thousand a week?" exclaimed Broadway. "Why, Bernhardt the Divine only got $1,000 a performance, wooden leg and all, and she wasn't playing every night."..."Five thousand a week!" echoed some. "Why, that gal can't speak a word of English"..."Neither can Sam Goldwyn," cracked a Broadwayite.

In the meantime, Broadway life moved along in its familiar groove— David Belasco went to Childs at 3 a.m. for his wheatcakes; night prowlers frequented Rector's, Shanley's, Reisenweber's and Jack's; celebrated folk of the town, including Enrico Caruso, A.L. Erlanger, Frohman and George M. Cohan, lunched daily at The Astor.

"Meet me at the Astor" was a catch phrase of New York society dur-ing the hotel's glory days, before the Great Depression cut annual Broad-way musical and play productions from 280 in 1928 to less than half that.

The Astor—erected by William Waldorf Astor, who built the origi-nal Waldorf before its Astoria annex (a structure more ornate than its original neighbor)—when it opened four years later had the good fortune to be run by Fred and William Muschenheim, who insisted on the finest food and amenities. They imported quail from Egypt and tripe from En-gland. These were not only served in The Astor's many wood-paneled restaurants but the hotel's roof garden, where water cascaded over a glass ceiling. Will Rogers lived and dined at The Astor long before the *Will Rogers Follies* hit the Palace Theatre. It was the time when he was starring in The Ziegfeld Follies, at the New Amsterdam Theatre on 42nd Street.

John J. Pershing (after whom Pershing Square was named just east of Grand Central Station), stayed there on the eve of taking command of the American Expeditionary Force in World War I.

The Astor ballroom, as big as its Broadway theater neighbors, was doubled in 1910. It was complete with a coffered vaulted ceiling, festooned with huge chandeliers. Years later, even the demolition of the 660-room Astor would prove a time-consuming engineering feat. "Her structural steel beams are of unusually heaving gauge," *The New York Times* reported.

In a city that had been the backdrop for countless political conventions and major news speeches, nothing was more dramatic than in 1916 when Republican Charles Evans Hughes went to bed in his Astor suite thinking he'd been elected President. California, voting later than most of the rest of the country, changed the election in favor of Woodrow Wilson. And when a reporter called to tell him, a valet of Hughes' replied, "The President has retired." With that the reporter reportedly shot back: "When he wakes tell him he's no longer President!"

My father, who was a *New York Sun* and *World Telegram & Sun* drama critic, ran the New York bureau of the *Atlanta Journal* in a room at The Astor for several years in the early 1920s.

The Park Central, situated uptown a bit on 56th Street and Seventh Avenue, was also the office and home of the late Jackie Gleason before his TV show moved to Miami. It was fitting that Jackie Gleason occupied the penthouse of the Statler, which was as huge in its own way as the master comedian. His suite, which was several thousand square feet, was painted a lemon meringue color. Most of his staff worked in the office until "The Great One" transferred lock, stock and barrel down to Miami on August 3, 1964.

The Belvedere at 319 West 48th Street was where Bing Crosby once lived. And Martin ("Marty") Richards, the Broadway producer who became world famous producing the movie *Chicago* with Richard Gere, Catherine Zeta-Jones and Renee Zellweger, lived at the Whitby, an apartment-hotel on West 45th Street. It was a place where, Mr. Richards recollects, "I could hear the trombone player next door as if he was playing right in my living room." But Mr. Richards, who married Johnson & Johnson heiress Mary Lea Johnson, also told me that "I'm sure my neighbor was just as offended by my singing!"

Song and dance man George M. Cohan is much associated with The Plaza. There the "Cohan corner" in the Oak Room was named after him. But he lived at the Savoy-Plaza across the street and when my father visited him one time there for a 1 p.m. appointment, Cohan, in a maroon dressing gown, was being given a hair cut by Fritz the barber who worked at "Chair 6" at the Astor Hotel. He'd been cutting Cohan's hair for years.

"Got a great title for a play the other day, kid," Cohan told my father. "Wonderful idea, as I was walking through Boston Common. 'Pigeons and People'—how do you like it? No idea for the play yet, but I'm 'foolin' around.'" "Foolin' around" was Cohan's way of saying he was working on something.

As I mentioned, smaller hotels with distinctive architectural features flourished on side streets in and near Times Square. One of these, Hotel Le Marquis was built in 1907 and has been utilized as a hotel ever since with the exception of the last 20 years. In early 2001, the Proprietor, Shimmie Hom, embarked on an ambitious plan to create a feeling of opulence and luxury in keeping with the neighborhood, using the original structure and name. The beautiful stone façade has been restored to its original splendor, and each room has been carefully created to provide the ultimate in travelers' comfort.

Times Square roof gardens really flowered before the days of air-cooled playhouses and movie theaters during the hot summer months when Broadway was virtually shut down and when summer stock theater, from the sandy beaches of Cape Cod and the Maine coast to the hills and valleys of Pennsylvania and Virginia, was at its zenith. There was Oscar Hammerstein's Paradise Roof Garden atop his Victoria Theatre on the site of the current New Victory Theatre at 42nd Street and Seventh Avenue. Madison Square Garden at Madison Square boasted one of the most popular and gained international infamy because it was where Harry K. Thaw shot architect Stanford White in a jealous rage over the "girl in the Swing," the beautiful Evelyn Nesbit. But, certainly, one of the most elaborate and beautiful roof gardens sat atop the Astor. Festooned with glass and hanging gardens, it had restaurants and a dance floor and its orchestra played into the wee hours of the summer nights. With the advent of Prohibition, it and others closed and were used only for occasional weddings and summer parties. While the Astor couldn't stop guests from having liquor in their rooms, it wasn't served during Prohibition in the hotel's restaurants or its roof. Smaller, upscale hotels like the Vanderbilt at Park Avenue and 34th Street, got top dollar for penthouse suites with elaborate gardens. Enrico Caruso had such a suite at the Vanderbilt, after living at the Knickerbocker became too much like living in a fishbowl with all his fans hanging on his every move. The Knickerbocker's architecture remarkably resembled that of the Plaza, designed by Henry J. Hardenbergh.

In its formative years, the Knickerbocker boasted prices undercutting hotels along Fifth and Madison Avenues. "A Fifth Avenue Hotel at Broadway prices," as that advertisement boasted. But if bellboys brought liquor to the rooms of guests at even the swankiest hotel, some Broadway roustabouts made their own brand of gin in their bathrooms.

Prohibition doomed the Knickerbocker Hotel because it depended heavily on its enormous restaurant and food concession to turn a profit. Likewise, its Times Square neighbors like Shanley's restaurant on 43rd Street and Broadway, closed several years later. Peter Shanley, one of five Shanley brothers who ran the restaurant, also called the "lobster palace," later said he lost a half million dollars when Shanley's closed. He then ran the bar at the Hotel Commodore which boasted it was the biggest bar in North America. Asked in 1936 by a reporter if Prohibition had anything to do with he and his brothers deciding to shut Shanley's, he shot back, "Did it have anything to do with the others deciding to retire?!"

My father and several of his wilder newspaper colleagues lived at the Lincoln, occupying a tower suite facing east toward the Paramount Building and New York Times Building on 43rd Street. Armed with the brew, one night they tried to shoot the hands off the Paramount clock.

The Edison Hotel was built as a direct result of the blockbuster success of *The Green Pastures*. Forty-seventh Street, which up to then had been comprised mostly of ramshackle buildings and tenement houses, almost overnight was redeveloped on the strength of *The Green Pastures*. The Edison went on to become a major venue for big bands.

"The Lincoln was followed by a few other smaller hotels in the Modernist manner in the Times Square area, including Schwartz & Gross's 1928 Hotel Victoria, at the northeast corner of Seventh Avenue and Fifty-first Street, Herbert J. Krapp's 1930 Hotel Edison, 228 West Forty-seventh Street with its vertically ribbed brick façade and its Modern French lobby purportedly based on the new Casino at Nice and Emery Roth's 650-room Hotel Dixie at 251 West Forty-second Street of 1930," the book *1900* notes. "It was also followed by one large, particularly uninventive hostelry, Gronenberg & Leuchtag's 1927 Park Central Hotel.... The thirty-one-story, 1,600-room Park Central, occupying the block front on the west side of Seventh Avenue between Fifty-fifth and Fifty-sixth Streets, was little more than a workmanlike exercise—a piece of urban infill whose interior was brightened by Willy Pogany's murals in the American Colonial room depicting the progression of American history from the early settlers to the present and into the immediate future."

Another interesting chapter in Manhattan hotel history was located near Times Square at 41st and Broadway, at the old address (albeit not the current address of) 1400 Broadway, on the east side of Broadway. No longer standing and demolished in the 1950s, with a Starbucks in its place on the street level today, it was known as The Hotel Calvert.

This seven-story structure was alternatively known as The Hotel Aberdeen. It served as both a hotel and an office building since about the turn of the century. The street entrance from Broadway had elaborate striped awnings.

Today if one looks carefully to the top of, and to the left of the early 1960s style grayish office building now on top of the Starbucks, one can make out a fireplace. In the nineteen-teens, it was The Hotel Knickerbocker. Today the façade of the office building is covered with advertising banners.

My father arrived in NYC from Savannah in 1919. Over the years he became friendly with a touring producer who made a lot of money by taking hit Broadway shows and then sending them out on tour to different cities throughout the United States. Oscar Edward Wee ("Harry" to his friends) was born in Janesville, Wisconsin in 1881 to a prosperous Norwegian-American family. The name Wee (Wei) in Norwegian is interesting in itself since it traverses many different ethnicities. The name exists in the Caucasian, Polynesian and Asian ethnic groups. Most likely the six-foot-three Wee's maternal ancestors were either Polish or Italian, perhaps creating a link to the flourishing arts in those countries of the 15th and 16th centuries.

Wee arrived in Manhattan in 1900 and had his offices as well as his residence on the seventh floor of the Calvert building. One of his early partners was the circus promoter Henry Clay Lambert. His daughter was the famed fashion publicist Eleanor Lambert Berkson who passed on in 2003 at nearly 100 years old.

From there Wee himself and later with partners, would send acting troupes throughout the country. Generally his actress wife, whose stage name was Louise Price, would go out with the group as the headliner. Cast members would double as electricians, carpenters, etc. This went on for years. Wee and his wife lived lavishly, residing in numerous New York hotels including The Waldorf. Photographs of his wife in costume were taken by the famed theater photographer Otto Sarony's studios.

By 1937, Wee had been partnered for a number of years with a European immigrant named J.J. Leventhal and Wee wanted to try his hand at Broadway. To the dismay of Leventhal, he chose a play by an author who nine years earlier had a successful book called *The Gangs of New York*. His name was Herbert Asbury (1889-1963).

By now my father was having weekly conversations with Wee to get the latest information from him about Broadway happenings. The team of Wee and Leventhal was alternately known as running the "Subway Circuit," so called because at this time many of these road plays appeared around the tri-state area, that is, in regions accessible by mass transit.

Wee also wanted to produce one of Asbury's few fiction works known as *The Devil of Pei Ling*. It was a murder mystery with occult elements tossed in. Leventhal was against the play fearing it would be a failure. Fulfilling this prediction, it ran only twelve performances at the Adelphi Theater at the site of the current New York Hilton. One actor listed in the program was Robert Shayne, later known to television viewers as Inspector Henderson on the Superman television series. My father wrote extensively about Wee in one of his "Broadway After Dark" column on May 12, 1934.

Fittingly, on December 12, 2002, at the Ziegfeld Theater across from the Hilton, Martin Scorsese's film *Gangs of New York* had its world premiere. Among the participants was Asbury's 92 year-old widow Edith Evans Asbury. One can just picture Asbury and Wee sizing up the situation for what they both thought would be a successful run.

The Roosevelt, which opened in 1924, and the Lincoln, now called the Milford Plaza and at one time called the Manhattan with its famous Playbill Bar, "employed motifs from the Colonial and Federal era, which Matlack Price saw as the most fitting architectural tribute possible to Roosevelt (the President) and as a stylistic ideal worthy of preservation," Messeurs. Stern, Gilmartin and Mellins write in *1900*.

Named for President Theodore Roosevelt, The Roosevelt was featured in such films as *The French Connection* and *Quiz Show*. The Roosevelt is most often remembered for big band leader Guy Lombardo's New Year's Eve "Auld Lang Syne" broadcasts. One of the four major "railroad" hotels, it was linked to Grand Central with an underground tunnel connecting the hotel to the train station. Today, the 1013-room Roosevelt still boasts a life-size bronze relief of its Rough Rider namesake.

In October, 2003, a man lost a diamond ring, the engagement ring he intended to propose to his fiancée with, in a taxi on the way to the Roosevelt. The hotel bought him a new ring equivalent to the £1,000 he paid for the one which was never recovered.

When it came to big bands, the Roosevelt came in second only to the Hotel Pennsylvania. "Glenn Miller owned the Hotel Pennsylvania," famed radio music nostalgia host Danny Styles told me. "It was his hotel."

Stewart F. Lane, the Tony Award-winning Broadway producer, theater owner and director tells the hilarious story of producing a "small musical"—only "a million dollars or so" at the Edison Theatre which had been The Edison Hotel's grand ballroom and once again is today. "It was opening night and we had all the critics in and all of a sudden the fire alarm went off and the fire department was conducting a test of the alarm system and it's my opening night. Well, I went to the captain and said, 'you've got some nerve conducting a test on my opening night. I've got all the critics in, *The New York Times*, the *Post*, the TV critics.' Well, he just gave me the kind of stare that goes right through you. I got the message. I could see I wasn't getting anywhere that way. So I tried 'nice'—begging for them to stop. That didn't work either. They said they weren't testing the alarm in the theater but in the hotel and they were all connected to one system and it would take another five minutes. Some critics got up and left. My director was crying and said he'd never work in this town again—and he never has. And when they finally got them to stop the damage was done and they killed us."

Irwin Chanin, an engineer as well as a developer, had cut his teeth building the Majestic, Royale and other Broadway playhouses before beginning work on the 1400-room Lincoln. A profile of him in the *New Yorker* said he "worked night and day on plans, details. He drew pictures himself of the kind of furniture he wanted in the lobby…sofas and chairs, the curves and angles of which represented the roofs and bridges of the city. He designed one frieze to show the shadow of a line of skyscrapers falling across a street, and another the motif of which is the tire of a Mack truck. He had lamps made to look like safes and fountains like an office building. He wasn't satisfied with making details; he sometimes worked even on the material of the decorations, grabbing the brush out of a painter's hand to show him what he wanted. Trying to find a detail that will tell something about Irwin Chanin, I can only say what has been said of many businessmen: that he has most of the characteristics of a competent artist. Buildings to him are ideas, at once more concrete and more abstract than they are to other people."

1900 notes that the nearby Picadilly, with 600 rooms and the 700-room Paramount, located on "comparatively inconspicuous side street locations…were no match for the vast, prominently located Hotel Lincoln of 1928, which the Chanin organization developed on the east side of Eighth Avenue between 44th and 45th Streets. It was originally concocted in a somewhat Spanish style by Herbert J. Krapp, who designed the Theatre Masque and the Majestic and Royale theaters for the Chanins.

"The Chanins believe that the audience comfort that was to be found in the motion-picture palaces spreading across the land was lacking in many of the existing legitimate houses, and they sought to catch up with the times," my father wrote in his Broadway theater history *Matinee Tomorrow*. "They adopted the stadium or amphitheater style of design for two of their largest houses; they provided large and beautiful foyers."

After having weathered new celebrity in the 1940s and '50s as part of the wartime and post-World War II theatrical boom, the Astor fell on hard times in the 1960s as did the Claridge, formerly The Rector, across Broadway. "Naughty, bawdy 42nd Street," as the song in the musical *42nd Street* goes, became naughtier and bawdier. A midway in the 1940s, with burlesque and penny arcades, it had transformed by the mid-1960's into the world's single biggest collection of peep shows.

"Forty-second Street will never change during my lifetime," the late veteran press agent Harvey Sabinson was fond of saying to me and everyone else. I was living at the Lambs Club, housed in an elegant Stanford White-designed building on 44th Street almost directly across from the Hudson Theatre in the late 1960's and early 1970's before going to Boston and taking a job on *The Christian Science Monitor*, and 44th Street was one of the most disreputable streets in all of the Times Square area. The Hudson had become a porn palace and the venerable Belasco featured the nudie musical *Oh, Calcutta!* Prostitutes plied their trade in a ramshackle hotel at 44th Street and Sixth Avenue and, at times, at what was then known as the 123 Hotel, at 123 West 44th Street.

All that began to change in the late 1980s after Disney announced plans to renovate the New Amsterdam in 1994. A promising new era began—the more cynical saying the start of the Disneyfication of Times Square. One can only wonder what would Damon Runyun have thought of this startling transformation of his old haunt.

The majestic Astor Hotel, the patrician Hotel Rector, later called the Claridge, may be long gone but even now you can step back into time at the Gotham Hospitality Group's four hotels. The Hotel Wales at 1295 Madison Avenue (at 92nd Street) was there when Andrew Carnegie was having breakfast in his mansion overlooking Central Park two blocks away. Its sister hotel, the Mansfield, was a favorite of those dining at Delmonico's at 44th Street and Fifth Avenue in the 1920's. Close your eyes as you leave the richly ornamented Victorian lobby of the Wales and you could be back in the days of the horse-drawn carriages and maybe even catch a glimpse of the young Alfred G. Vanderbilt driving his team of horses on a Sunday afternoon.

Louis Korn designed the nine-story Wales Hotel, first called the Hotel Chastaignary when it opened in 1901. It replaced some six one-story buildings. It's a block and a half from the Cooper-Hewett Museum, built by Andrew Carnegie as his magnificent home on Fifth Avenue and 91st Street, which Carnegie liked to call "the Highlands of New York," and later just called the Carnegie Hill area. The Chastaignary opened a year before the Algonquin, making it one of the oldest continuously operated hotels in the city.

Lo Van der Valk, president of Carnegie Hill Neighbors and a man devoted to preserving the architectural integrity of the neighborhood, believes that some of Mr. Carnegie's friends or perhaps even relatives may have stayed at the Wales, though there is no evidence to support this such as hotel records. It's questionable whether Carnegie himself ever set foot there.

The owners are Hardin Capital, based in Atlanta, which bought it in November, 2002. "We did a major renovation, like $3 million in 2000 with the previous owner," manager Janice Perna-Nicholas told me. "We went through all the guest rooms and did all the bathrooms over. The two things in the lobby that are original are the ceiling and the floor. It's still not quite done. We're still waiting for some more furniture down there, more art work. This is a very special place. It's very unique in its design; it's charming. It's peaceful. People that appreciate dark wood molding, people that appreciate the style and the décor come back and back and back. My repeat business is about 45 percent. This is their hotel.

"As a general manager it starts at the top. I get involved in total customer service and it trickles down. That's the difference in an historic hotel. It would be the charm, the character, the peacefulness. Here you've got the location; the great building and the great service...87 rooms and suites. We have 41 suites. Not quite 50 percent. [The executive suite I stayed in, by way of price comparison, rents for up to $479 a night from September to December.] There are many celebrities who stay here because it's private; it's residential and many newscasters in Manhattan stay here; have their families stay here."

The Park Central, may be a swell place for families, too, but was connected to at least one notorious incident.For years, stories evolved about who killed the notorious organized crime figure, Albert Anastasia. The true murderers of Albert Anastasia have never been caught, but one thing we do know is that on the morning of October 25, 1957, Anastasia arrived for a haircut in the barber shop of the Park Central Hotel. At least two barbershop staffers were in attendance, the owner, Arthur Grasso and a barber, John Arbissi. Whatever did follow certainly proved to be too close of a shave for Mr. Anastasia. Some design features of the hotel still remain today that played a role that fateful day. The parking garage is still in place. It was through this entry that the assailants gained access to the basement barbershop.

The Carter Hotel on 43rd Street, between Broadway and Eight Avenue, was originally called The Dixie Hotel. Like many of the hotels in and around the Rialto, it started out as a first-class hotel but in the 50s and 60s became run down. Yet even in the 40s it was a magnet for upscale tourists visiting Broadway. It was also the scene for some high level counterintelligence activities.

"My father told me the story that during the war (World War II) he was a counterintelligence agent for the United States," recalled Robert Shanley, chairman of the New York Food & Hotel Management School. Mr. Shanley's father, Jack Shanley, went on to a career as a reporter and editor with *The New York Times*. Mr. Shanley, by the way is directly related to the Shanley Brothers who opened the Shanley's Restaurants in the 1890s, the biggest one being Shanley's at Broadway and 43rd Street on the site of what is now the Paramount Building on Broadway and 43rd Street.

"The first year or two of the war he was under cover here in New York; he was a plain-clothes military intelligence agent," Mr. Shanley told me. "And the Dixie Hotel was a rendezvous point for passing on intelligence information. There was a room at the Dixie Hotel. My father had been a copyboy at the *Times* before the war and then joined the military and then went back to the *Times* after the war. He said nobody knew that the Dixie was this meeting place for agents passing on important information during the war years. The Dixie was a very anonymous place to pass on counterintelligence.

"He was doing a lot of surveillance of German saboteurs. My brother actually has one of his surveillance reports. It gets almost silly where they are following a suspected German spy and they hop-scotch in cabs. The surveillance ends when my father and his partner can't find a cab and the German does. And where the room in the Dixie Hotel came into the picture is that nobody knew that that was where they met to pass information. It was one room and he just went in there and gave his report to a counter-intelligence official. And my brother reminded me the other day that J.D. Salinger worked with my father. They became good friends. We're not sure if J.D. Salinger worked with my father in Manhattan or if it was overseas. My brother seems to recollect that he worked in surveillance during the early part of the war. I remember my father telling me that in one of the short stories Salinger wrote he used my father as a character. Who would have thought that J.D. Salinger was in counter-intelligence?"

I asked Robert Shanley to see if he could find any reference to J.D. Salinger himself reporting to the Dixie. Alas, Mr. Shanley could find nothing in his father's notes or writings that Mr. Salinger ever carried on his espionage duties at the Hotel Dixie. "My father and Salinger knew each other in India. Actually, the only reason he even talked to my father was that they were both writers. My father might have been doing stories without a by-line before the war. Salinger was not friendly to many people (during the war)."

But if Salinger never reported to the secret room at the Dixie he did write about old hotels and an "Old man Shanley" in "Pretty Mouth and Green My Eyes," which was published in the *New Yorker* in July 14, 1951. Robert Shanley believes it was "Old man Shanley" because his father was balding in his late '20's, and looked older than the younger men like himself in the war.

Part of the *New Yorker* story goes this way:

"How'd you make out today?" the gray-haired man repeated. "How'd the case go?"

"Oh, Christ! I don't know. Lousy. About two minutes before I'm all set to start my summation, the attorney for the plaintiff, Lissberg, trots in this crazy chambermaid with a bunch of bed sheets as evidence—bedbug stains all over them. Christ!"

"So what happened" You lose?" asked the gray-haired man, taking another drag on his cigarette.

"You know who was on the bench? Mother Vittorio. What the hell that guy has against me, I'll never know. I can't even open my mouth and he jumps all over me. You can't reason with a guy like that. It's impossible."

The gray-haired man turned his head to see what the girl was doing. She had picked up the ashtray and was putting it between them. "You lose, then, or what?" he said into the phone.

"What?"

"I said, Did you lose?"

"Yeah. I was gonna tell you about it. I didn't get a chance at the party, with all the ruckus. You think Junior'll hit the ceiling? Not that I give a good goddam, but what do you think? Think he will?"

With his left hand, the gray-haired man shaped the ash of his cigarette on the rim of the ashtray. "I don't think he'll necessarily hit the ceiling, Arthur," he said quietly. "Chances are very much in favor, though, that he's not going to be overjoyed about it. You know how long we've handled those three bloody hotels? Old man Shanley himself started the whole -"

"I know, I know. Junior's told me about it at least fifty times. It's one of the most beautiful stories I ever heard in my life. All right, so I lost the goddam case. In the first place, it wasn't my fault. First, this lunatic Vittorio baits me all through the trial. Then this moron chambermaid starts passing out sheets full of bedbugs."

"It was very hard for my father at the time because these guys (counter-intelligence agents) all wore suits and he wasn't allowed to tell anyone he was in the military," Mr. Shanley said. "He had been a copyboy at the *Times* before the War and he basically had to pretend he was a civilian and that was very tough when all the other guys were going overseas. And he said it was very hard not to tell people he was in counter-intelligence. He said when he went to the Dixie Hotel it was as if he was a businessman. He would simply go to the room and it was very anonymous and nobody knew who he was. They had typed up information and were given new assignments."

To producer Oscar Hammerstein, father of lyricist Oscar Hammerstein II, goes the distinction of helping rename the Rialto the Great White Way when in 1898 he illuminated the marquee of his Olympia Theater with hundreds of light bulbs. Other theaters with equally bright lights followed in quick succession.

"By the end of the first decade of the new century, 'Broadway' no longer merely defined a Manhattan location but a national industry," Marc Eliot says in his illuminating history *Down 42nd Street*. "To accommodate its ever-growing New York audiences, new and more glamorous playhouses were built along Broadway, with ever-fancier restaurants and hotels filling out the newly re-named Times Square district. The most glamorous of these, the Astor, opened its doors in 1904, as did the equally fashionable Knickerbocker Hotel, located on the south side of 42nd Street, to the south east of the new Times Tower. The Knickerbocker quickly became the essential eating, drinking and rooming establishment in the giddy atmosphere that now enveloped the neighborhood."

Of course, in the 1960's and 1970's, Times Square was to experience urban blight of the worst sort; hotels along the Rialto became ghostly counterparts of the once grand hotels of Atlantic City, poised on the edge of an economic and social revolution. In Atlantic City, gambling would forever change the character of the seaside resort; in New York, pornography and big business were the odd bed fellows which forever changed the character of the one-time greatest theatrical Mecca in the world.

Today, one-time ghosts of themselves like The Ansonia have survived beautifully but The Astor, Rector and The Metropol south of 42nd Street are gilded memories only. The Casablanca, formerly Rosoff's and the (new) Metropol, survives and had the distinction, for a time, of boasting the highest hotel prices in Times Square.

A century earlier, peaceful residential Longacre Square was invaded by the *The New York Times*, a leading media company of its era, and was transformed into the legendary theater district of Times Square. At the end of the last century, Disney Inc., a leading media company of its era, moved in and had a similar transformative impact, but what the new Times Square will ultimately look like is still up in the air. At least they haven't yet renamed it Mickey Square.

CHAPTER 6
THE ANSONIA

Enrico Caruso, Florence Ziegfield, Lilly Pons, Arturo Toscanini and Theodore Dreiser lived at the Ansonia, built by William Earl Dodge on a 44,000 square foot site at Broadway and 73rd Street. Working with French architect Paul Emile (E.M.) Dubov, who designed the Soldiers' and Sailors Monument on Riverside Drive, the 17-story Ansonia was even more wildly lavish than the Henry J. Hardenbergh-designed Plaza Hotel. But unlike The Plaza, which took only two years to build, construction on The Ansonia, which began on November 15, 1899, wasn't completed until April 19, 1904, nearly five years later. Like The Plaza, The Ansonia boasted a palm garden but unlike its more celebrated competitor it also had a trellised roof garden.

In the hotel's heyday from 1904 to the advent of the Great Depression the rich and famous primarily from the worlds of music and theater lived in palatial splendor unequaled in a New York apartment hotel with bay-windowed round parlors and oval hallways and servants rooms in individual apartments—not in the eaves of the roof as was the case at the Dakota or even The Plaza, but on the same level with their employers.

The Ansonia's cavernous lobby, banked by richly textured mahogany paneling and ornate ceiling, was reminiscent of the fanciful digs of the erstwhile silent screen diva in *Sunset Boulevard*.

"The Ansonia transformed French prototypes into a veritable skyscraper," according to *1900*. The hotel lobby also boasted a fountain with spigots spouting water which cascaded down either side of it.

Eugene Walter, whose play *Paid in Full*, catapulted him to the front ranks of American dramatists, lived at the Ansonia, which took its place beside the Gotham on West 55th Street as one of the premier "apartment hotels" in the city. Like short story writer and novelist Jack London, Walter had been a gold prospector and adventurer before venturing into drama. His realistic plays set the stage for Eugene O'Neill's even greater realism. Walter, who had made millions, died in Hollywood in the 1940's leaving a substantial body of work. While living at the Ansonia, Walter would walk his big dog, a white bull terrier, in the Ansonia's special "dog room," the only room of its kind I've ever heard of. Despite his success and celebrity, the hotel ordered Walter to leave the hotel in 1908 because his big dog was barking and chasing guests.

Along with the Ansonia, the Dorilton (at 71st Street and Broadway) helped transform upper Broadway into a kind of American Champs-Elysee, with its Park Avenue-like ultra broad streets. While the Dorilton would remain an enclave for upper-middle-class Westsiders, the Ansonia went the way, in the 1960's, of its Times Square counterpart—the Claridge Hotel, formerly called The Rector, at 44th Street and Broadway.

William Earl Dodge (W.E.D.) Stokes used part of his inheritance to build the Ansonia. Stokes hired architect Stanford White to design the Ansonia, named for one of Stokes' relatives. He himself lived in the hotel's penthouse and from time to time provided tenants with fresh eggs from chickens he kept on the roof.

Robert Reinhart, a resident of the Ansonia for 44 years from 1913 to 1954, wrote in a by-line piece for *The New York Times* that "The gracious halls, despite their cushioned carpets, were the playing fields of resident moppets when they managed to escape supervision. We biked, roller skated." He remembered playing with sisters named Constance, Barbara and Joan Bennett, children of Adrienne Morrison and actor Richard Bennett. These sisters went on to distinguished stage and screen careers.

"During World War I, when I was in elementary school, I canvassed the building after classes, selling Liberty Bonds. I recollect calling on Billie Burke (Mrs. Florence Ziegfeld) and Mae Murray, the silent screen star. In post-World War I days, the large lobby was filled every evening with baseball stars. Almost all the Yankees and many of the visiting players lived there when the games were played in New York."

"There was the often-married Peggy Hopkins Joyce, and Dagmar Godowsky, a sultry film actress and the musician, who sashayed through the lobby in dazzling evening gowns. Jack Dempsey and his wife, Estelle Taylor were tenants."

Arturo Toscanini became principal conductor for the Metropolitan Opera in late 1908 and lived at the Ansonia Hotel for the next eight years. According to *The Letters of Arturo Toscanini*, compiled by Harvey Sachs, Toscanini wrote one friend that he led a rather staid life at the hotel. "When I have nothing to do at the theater I stay home. I study, and from time to time I read in English."

The hotel had some highly unusual unscheduled events over the years. Once in 1916, German forces tried to blow it up, according to William Burn's book, *The Eagle's Eye*, when American naval officers were at a dance in the grand ballroom.

Like other wealthy families who could afford their pick of the better apartment hotels, the Reinharts had fun with maids of their day. He recalled that he and his siblings "deliberately stayed in bed waiting" for one maid's entrance. "She would dramatically command, 'Get up, you bastards!' If we did not move quickly enough she would rip away the sheets."

In the early 1970's preservationists feared the Ansonia was on the verge of being razed for another nondescript high-rise apartment building. The late actress Geraldine Fitzgerald and many other entertainers gathered to protest what they thought would be the imminent destruction of the hotel.

"When I came to this country from Ireland," Ms. Fitzgerald told a reporter, "this was where I first stayed. It was a beautiful welcome to America. It is still beautiful."

The Ansonia hadn't yet been formally designated a landmark by the Landmarks Preservation Commission, which would have rendered it virtually impossible to raze. It was considered "an economic liability" by its owners, the Ansonia Holding Corporation.

It also housed the notorious sex club, Plato's Retreat, which didn't endear The Ansonia to its West End Avenue neighbors.

In 1980, Paul Goldberger, then architecture critic of *The New York Times*, wrote of the Ansonia that the lobby "has deteriorated so badly it looks like the vestibule of a skid row hotel."

Things started looking up for the hotel when Ansonia Associates took over its management in 1978 and put on a new roof to stop leaks and began slowly renovating apartments. Mr. Goldberger cautioned the new owners and managers to renovate The Ansonia "with the utmost care." Undoubtedly, these and other preservationist admonitions, coupled with the boom in Manhattan real estate during the 1980's, helped return the

Ansonia to its current status as one of the most sought after residential buildings on Manhattan's West Side. Who knows, one of these days maybe even the Yankees might come back.

CHAPTER 7
THE PLAZA HOTEL

My father's life at The Plaza revolved around the theater and it symbolized The Plaza's own association with Broadway and show business. So it seems appropriate to include the entire text of a piece he wrote for *Collier's* magazine about a week at The Plaza—in his case a fairly typical week:

> "Having galloped through another of her vastly engaging performances as Gigi at the Fulton, Audrey Hepburn gorges herself on Stork Club ice cream. She declines host Sherman Billingsley's gift of champagne but accepts a lipstick, flashes brown eyes that turn greenish, and chatters: 'Oh, I thought I was such a blooming flop on the opening night, but then, at the end, the audience was wonderful. Jolly wonderful.' Miss Hepburn is not bad herself.
>
> "Tuesday, Rosalind Russell, staying at the Pierre Hotel before going on tour, charms with eyes and hands as she talks. 'Plans?' she asks. 'I want to tour in *Bell, Book and Candle* until spring, and come to Broadway in a new play in the fall.'
>
> "The next day, over a sea-food luncheon at the Gloucester House, Katharine Cornell, a star for three decades, chants: 'I was nervous as a witch before *The Constant Wife* opened, but that's nothing new. I've always been nervous. I was glad, however, to be coming back in something gay.'
>
> "On Thursday, I wandered up to Gracie Square, near where the mayor of the city lives, for a talk with Alfred Lunt and Mrs. Lunt-Lynn Fontanne—in their charming,

71

narrow (16 feet), exquisitely decorated East End Avenue townhouse. They bought the place only after many rent-paying years.

"If you're still along with me, I went on Friday to the soda fountain in Jack Nicholas' crossroads store in Grand Central Station with the distractingly profane and enormously talented Barbara Bel Geddes, who has that scrubbed, bobby-sox look. Her performance as the outspoken virgin in *The Moon Is Blue* is one of the delights of the New York theater. The play will earn a million.

"On Saturday, I walk out upon the Avenue, watching the out-of-towners who come to visit my town. I finish out the day in paying a call upon one of these visitors, Ginger Rogers, who found a play (*Love and Let Love*) and lost it on Broadway last year. Then to the theater to see Gertrude Lawrence in the play of her career, *The King and I*, and to speak a moment with her, backstage. And so home to the big hotel on the edge of Theatertown.

"On Sundays I scorn the subway and get into my car to deliver my Monday copy to the *World-Telegram & Sun*. Then, frequently, I drop in at Luchow's in Union Square for German pancakes-and then drive on back to my midtown acreage, where I know people, many people.

"It's all about like it used to be in Savannah, Georgia, where I was born. Just like it is now in Register, Georgia, where I have a farm. Just like it might be in Santa Fe, which is on my dream schedule for the years to come."

As I said, my father actually lived in 29 hotels in New York, including the Waldorf-Astoria and The Plaza, where he and my stepmother, Rebecca Morehouse, lived for those 11 years.

It was at the St. Regis at 5th Avenue and 55th Street in around 1904 that Bernhard ("Ben") Beinecke, who had amassed massive Manhattan stockyards and Canadian developer Henry Black were having breakfast one morning lamenting that they couldn't find the cash necessary, a tidy sum of $12 million, to build The Plaza when a voice from the next table, apparently overhearing their conversation, bellowed that "If you get Fred Sterry to manage The Plaza, you can count on me for all the money you need."

This was John W. ("Bet-a-Million") Gates, who had been living at the old Waldorf-Astoria at 34th Street and Fifth Avenue on the current site of the Empire State Building. Gates would take a bet on anything, like which raindrop would reach the bottom of a windowpane first and if he were alive today would bet on just how long—how many months or days—Liza Minnelli, who got married to someone who had been a rather obscure producer, would stay married. Anyway, Gates was in the deal after Beineke and Black hired Sterry, who had managed the Homestead Inn in Virginia. So the old Plaza—there had been an old Plaza built in 1890 which was a bit of a bust—was torn down in 1905 and work began on one of the wonders of New York.

Charles Melville Hayes, general manager of the Grand Trunk Pacific Railway, was scheduled to stay at the Plaza when he went down on the *Titanic*. He was on his way to the opening of the $2 million Chateau Laurier in Ottawa, Canada, scheduled to open on April 26, 1912 but he and his party, and presumably furniture on its way to the Laurier, went down on the *Titanic* on April 12. The Laurier's grand opening was postponed to June of the same year.

Speaking of bear country, I've told you a little about the bear who lived at The Plaza, who was asked to leave my father's suite because he nipped the maids' feet every time they tried to clean the kitchen or bathroom. But The Plaza has had more than its share of animals. Legendary public relations man Lee Solters, who represented Frank Sinatra and many others, was employed by the hotel at one time when he registered a "Miss Ella Phant" in a park view suite. No one would have given it a second thought when in walked Miss Phant, with a bright pink bow. Yes, she was a baby elephant. The front desk clerk became so upset he demanded she register in her own handwriting whereupon Solters leaned over and clued him into the publicity stunt for the circus, which had come to town. Although Miss Phant was whisked up to a suite she later came down the service elevator, where a scrumptious bale of hay awaited her.

When William Beinecke used to visit his grandfather, Bernhard, the first owner of The Plaza, he'd often stand on a small balcony overlooking Fifth Avenue to see a parade and other sights and sounds. "I didn't grow up with the feeling that The Plaza belonged to my family; it was simply a place where my grandparents lived," he wrote in his autobiography, *Through Mem'ry's Haze*.

He also talks about his grandfather, Johann, in the book. Johann drove a butcher's wagon, "bought out the company and became a titan of American industry." He was, Mr. Beinecke adds, the "force behind the construction of The Manhattan Hotel in New York and The Copley Plaza in Boston. The jewel in the crown was the present Plaza Hotel in Manhattan, which he opened in 1907."

It's interesting to note that The Manhattan, which was razed to make room for the Sperry & Hutcheson building, looked remarkably like The Plaza though it was smaller in size and in the number of rooms.

The Plaza, though not an immediate financial success, eventually became the hotel equivalent of the boxing champion of the world. One by one guests began leaving The Waldorf for The Plaza. "Then one explosive day the dike seemed to burst when thirty-two families packed up and left the old Waldorf to join the northward migration to The Plaza," Albin Pasteur Dearing wrote in *The Elegant Inn*, the story of the first Waldorf-Astoria. "They were the very core of the Waldorf's prominent social and political patronage from Chicago, Baltimore, Cleveland and Pittsburgh."

When it opened The Plaza advertised single rooms at $2.50 a night "with bath." Two- bedroom, two-bath suites began at $16 a night.

Children and pets play almost as much importance, at least for me personally, as does The Plaza's more illustrious guests. My father kept that bear at The Plaza for a short time before moving to a family farm in Georgia but not before redecorating the kitchen. And in an era—the 1950's—when it wasn't against the law to keep wild animals at home, I had a lion cub for several months until he died of pneumonia.

Which brings up the most well-trained pet ever to live at The Plaza— a Boston bulldog named Captain and owned by Mrs. Benjamin Kirkland of Philadelphia. Most every evening Captain left the area of the hotel safe holding a Russian leather jewel case between his teeth. He was tailed by Mrs. Kirkland's maid and, occasionally, a Pinkerton security guard.

Eloise, the fictional six-year old who lived at The Plaza may have had her own menagerie of pets including Skipperdee, but it was Eloise herself who turned the most heads—at least in Kay Thompson's "Eloise" storybooks illustrated by Hilary Knight. She'd slide down banisters, take a bath with her turtle and threaten to—but never did, pour water down the mail chutes. Knight told me, "Most people when they speak about the book *Eloise* refer to it as 'Eloise at the Plaza'—and to me that's proof of the inseparable connection between the two."

Hard as they try, no one has quite solved the mystery of the origin of Eloise. Some say Kay Thompson's inspiration for Eloise was Liza Minnelli, who lived at the hotel with her mother. Employees say she roller-skated if not in the lobby at least out on Central Park South in front of The Plaza. Regardless of whether this was true or not the two became close. Thompson was Liza's godmother and later Liza took care of Thompson in her waning years. But from my research and interviewing close friends of Thompson's, the inspiration for "Eloise" actually came from Thompson herself.

"I am Eloise, I am six!" Thompson herself would exclaim in a little girl voice when she was a dancer and was late for rehearsal and didn't want the director to explode.

Nevertheless, claims to the contrary that "Eloise" was the creation of this or that person continue. Once the hotel got a letter from a rather burly gentleman—a former musician at the hotel—who said, "Eloise is me!"

Enrico Caruso, the great Italian tenor, checked into the hotel shortly after it opened to see what all the fuss was about. He was vocalizing for an appearance at the Metropolitan Opera House when the buzzing of the "Magneta" clock on the marble fireplace—an almost inaudible buzzing—got to him. He suddenly lunged at it with a carving knife. Well, no one would have been the wiser if it had been the average clock but the hotel's magneta clocks were all linked together and his displeasure knocked all the clocks in the hotel out! These days he might have gone to jail. In those days they sent him a case of champagne.

The singer Hildegarde Neff would make waves some thirty years later. And even though the famed Persian Room had opened in 1934 she really put it on the map during World War II. She held café society spellbound and generations fell in love with her sultry voice and sense of humor. When young Congressman John F. Kennedy came to see the "incomparable Hildegarde," she slipped and fell flat on her face. A little dazed, she looked up at the dashing Congressman and said, "You see, I've fallen for you!"

Off-stage as well, Hildegarde, who is still with us in a nursing home in Manhattan at 95, maintained her sense of humor. Famed celebrity photographer Annie Lebowitz spent hours photographing Hildegarde for *Vogue* several years ago. When she finally got the right shot, she said, "Oh, Hildegarde, that's incredible!" And Lebowitz turned to Hildegarde's manager and said, "Isn't that incredible?!" And her manager, said, "Well, she's actually incomparable!" borrowing the common catch phrase about her. And with that Hildegarde, weakly piped up, "No, actually, she's uncomfortable!"

Cary Grant, who often stayed at the Plaza, as well as having acted some scenes of *North by Northwest* in the hotel, demanded prompt and attentive service. He once left a waiter and chef practically speechless by repeatedly asking where the fourth half of his English muffin was. After getting no response from the tongue-tied waiter, he charged downstairs and asked the chef, "What did you do with the fourth half?" "We use it for the base of Eggs Benedict," the stunned chef replied. Perhaps sensing the light comedy of a scene which could have come from one of his own movies, the star simmered down.

"I sang at the Persian Room," Kitty Carlisle Hart told me. The erstwhile Broadway and Hollywood star and former chairman of the New York State Council on the Arts was at the time sitting in her cavernous living room on Madison Avenue in the East 60s in Manhattan. "And I had the most terrible experience there that I've ever had in my whole life. The Persian Room of The Plaza was so chic. Everybody came. I got a brand new dress and I had everything so beautifully organized. And I was singing my first number and forgot the words. So I thought the orchestra would give me a chance to sing it again. But they went on to the second number! So, now I'm singing and I can't hear them. I'm so nervous. I'm singing one song and playing another. It was pandemonium. It was not my finest hour."

Ms. Hart, of course, was married to the late Broadway playwright Moss Hart, who wrote such classic plays with George S. Kaufman as *The Man Who Came to Dinner* and *George Washington Slept Here*. Before she married Hart she went out with George Gershwin. "George asked me to marry him," Ms. Hart told me. "He had the idea that it was time for him to get married. He wanted to marry a Jewish girl. But I was just starting out and wanted to get on with my career. We went dancing at El Morocco and we went to a prize fight and we walked in the park."

On her 96th birthday, Kitty Carlisle Hart played a week at Feinstein's at the Regency to sold-out crowds. Besides starring in *A Night at the Opera* with the Marx Brothers, she was in two films with Bing Crosby and well as Woody Allen's *Radio Days*. During the course of her show at the Regency in 2004 she told how she first met playwright Moss Hart, whom she later married. She'd been invited to a dinner party at Lillian Hellman's home and "during the course of the evening at Lillian's I was sitting on a sofa and Mr. Hart was sitting on the opposite sofa. I knew he had been to the South Pacific during World War II with his play *The Man Who Came to Dinner* to entertain the troops. I looked up at him and said, 'Moss, tell me about your trip to the South Pacific.' And we were married eight months later."

Financier Roy Neuberger is one of Miss Hart's current traveling companions. He celebrated his 100th birthday in July 2003, and has lived at the Pierre Hotel for many years amid some of his most cherished art treasures. Born in Bridgeport, Connecticut, on July 21, 1903, Mr. Neuberger used his ability to make money on Wall Street to finance his real passion for collecting art, a passion which grew out of living in Paris in the Twenties on an inheritance from his family. Weathering the Wall Street crash, he formed Neuberger & Berman with the late Robert Berman and the firm went on to manage some $55 billion annually. Mr. Neuberger used much of the money he made amassing one of the greatest private collections of contemporary art in the United States.

"When I was at the Plaza, there were some 'permanents' left," Tom List, who became general manager of the fabulous Woodstock (Vermont) Inn, told me. "In the late 1970s and early 1980s, Fannie Lowenstein was permanent, a Mr. Shapiro was a permanent. I think Fannie Lowenstein was a former dancer. She was a real character. She would come down to the front desk and bark at the staff."

Mr. List's dad was general manager of the Penn Garden Hotel and "when we lived at the Penn Garden (now the Southgate Tower across from Madison Square Garden) our terrace was on the 31st floor. Our suite number was 3104. So when I was seven years old I'd be playing with my matchbox cars on the terrace and I watched them dig for Madison Square Garden...the Penn Garden is now the Southgate Tower, a Manhattan East Hotel. The Statler Hilton was across the street which is now the Hotel Pennsylvania...Living in hotels—it spoils you. There is no doubt and it's great. My wife, Cindy, reminds me sometimes, 'Oh, Tom, just so you know, your laundry is not going to be folded anymore and brought to your room in a box—so get downstairs and get the laundry!'"

No one, not even Kay Thompson, has written more about The Plaza than playwright Neil Simon. In *Barefoot in the Park* starring Robert Redford and Jane Fonda. In *Plaza Suite*, starring Walter Matthau. Matthau, incidentally liked to stay at the Pierre. One morning he didn't get his coffee on time and called down to Sonja, the room service telephone operator, "Sonja, did you send to Sumatra for my coffee!?" In the serendipity world of the hotels we're talking about, Sonja was once a prosperous restaurateur who loved to dine The Plaza and Pierre. She went through a bad divorce before she was hired as a room service operator.

Simon said he could have called *Plaza Suite* "Waldorf Suite" but that "there was something about the hotel that was very romantic whereas I didn't feel that about other hotels."

He also spent his honeymoon with his first wife, Joan, at The Plaza. And wrote a lot of one play, *The Gingerbread Lady* in a small room at The Plaza in the four or five weeks his townhouse was being painted.

Part of the plot of *Plaza Suite* deals with a bride-to-be who has cold feet at the last minute. Real life weddings at The Plaza are more glamorous and sometimes stranger than fiction. Two-time Oscar nominee Sylvia Miles—you may remember her as the hooker in *Midnight Cowboy*—told me she was married in the "State Suite" of The Plaza and spent a two-night honeymoon there—and "The honeymoon was longer than the marriage."

On a more serious note, Michael Douglas and Catherine Zeta-Jones were, of course, married at The Plaza. Zeta-Jones said she chose The Plaza because it reminded her of the best in New York. Speaking of the State Suite, this is a series of rooms on the second floor of the hotel that are among its most sumptuous, with marble fireplaces and crystal chandlers. Now, they're function rooms for parties—I had my *Inside the Plaza* book party there. But one manager once had a devil of a time getting a tenant out of the State Suite. New York City law says that if you're paying your hotel bill and aren't breaking the law, a hotel can't evict you. Well, it seems this one lady, who was on a ridiculously low long term lease of $300 a month, would occasionally sit outside her suite and taunt the hotel management, sticking out her tongue like Eloise.

Stevie Wonder wasn't married at The Plaza but likes to stay in the same suite overlooking Central Park. After Ivana and Donald Trump took over the hotel in the late 1980's he told one of the managers that "something's different."

"I know, you're asking yourself how I know something is different," Wonder added, "because I can't see. I can *smell* the difference!"

You see, Ivana was a stickler for cleanliness. She personally showed the maids how to clean the rooms. And from her apartment high above Fifth Avenue she kept an eagle eye on the Fifth Avenue entrance of The Plaza. If she spotted a scrap of paper on the sidewalk she'd phone down to the doorman to pick it up!

Of course, when Donald Trump bought the hotel in the late 1980's his first order of business was to install his wife, Ivana, as president. Between them they gave it the celebrity status the Plaza always had long had, but which had started to fade during the Vietnam War. Trump sold it for less than he paid for it to Chairman Kwek of Millennium Hotels and Prince Alwaleed in the Spring of 1995.

I asked Ivana in mid-2003 if she would ever like to run a hotel again and she answered the question by explaining her management style.

"I've done it—I loved doing it," she told me. "I'm a natural manager. I love to manage. My love for running a hotel is basically an extension of running a household."

I interviewed Prince Alwaleed in early April 2000—he's the Saudi Prince who offered the families of New York City's World Trade Center victims $10 million (which Mayor Giuliani turned down because the Prince had criticized U.S. policy on Israel)—and found him to be not only articulate but someone with unabashed affection for The Plaza. He also lavished praise on his partner and co-owner of The Plaza, chairman Kwek. The prince confided to me that he felt very comfortable with Mr. Kwek overseeing the management of The Plaza. "Mr. Kwek is an incredible partner and I like him a lot. I keep in his hands completely the management of The Plaza."

"In the whole world I believe, as far as the hotel business is concerned, there are several icons," the prince continued. "For example, in the United States, on the East coast there's The Plaza and on the West coast there's the Fairmont in San Francisco. If you go to the Far East another icon is The Regent in Hong Kong and in France another icon is The George V and all these hotels I'm involved with them. So really to me to be involved with The Plaza is something very important to me...and our policy is to have special icons whenever we are involved in this industry."

"Do you enjoy staying at The Plaza when you're in New York?" I put to him. "Yes, I always stay at The Plaza when I'm in New York. In New York, I have this hotel. I have the Four Seasons and I also have the Pierre Hotel which is managed by Four Seasons (management company). But I always stay at The Plaza."

Asked if he brings his own chef with him he emphatically said, "Oh, no, no, no. We will use the food The Plaza has. I use a big area of the Palm Court as my office. We always do our transactions there. All my business is conducted there."

Alas, all good things, even at the Plaza, must come to an end. The Plaza was sold in August 2004 for $675 million to Elad Properties, NY, LLC. "The hotel needs renovation and I don't want to spend money anymore," explained Millennium chairman Kwek Leng Beng. He and Saudi

Prince Alwaleed bin Talal had purchased the Plaza from Donald Trump for an estimated $325 million in 1995. Plans call for many rooms and suites to be sold much like the Pierre or Carlyle with the remaining rooms rented to transients as always.

I talked to Gary Schweikert, general manager of the Plaza, the summer before 9/11 and he counted his blessings having been at both the Waldorf and Plaza. "I've been lucky enough to stay in the New York area where my family is located, having worked at the Waldorf, and I thought that it was such a magical place and having the honor to be here as well. It's hard to imagine what comes next." The Plaza and the Waldorf share the honors as America's if not the world's most famous hotels. "I had a friend who went on vacation in Hong Kong and I asked him to put 'the plaza Hotel, United States of America,' on the envelope," Tom Civitano, the Plaza's longtime vice-president of sales and marketing, told me. "And within 14 days of being postmarked it arrived at the Plaza."

Speaking of the romance of hotels, that old hotel buff F. Scott Fitzgerald celebrated romance at The Plaza in *The Great Gatsby* and *The Beautiful and the Damned*. Fitzgerald frequented the Grill Room even when he didn't have the money to stay at The Plaza. During Prohibition, he'd pay $7 a bottle for gin stored in a subbasement wine cellar of the hotel. Fitzgerald and his bride, the former Zelda Sayre, didn't spend their honeymoon at The Plaza, but it was a place the author practically worshipped and he helped immortalize it in his "Jazz Age" accounts.

During rehearsals for F. Scott's play, *The Vegetable*, which opened in November 20, 1923 starring veteran Broadway star Earnest Truex, the Fitzgeralds sometimes stayed at the Plaza when Scott didn't want to commute to Great Neck, Long Island. But as Sara Mayfeld writes in her book, "Exiles from Paradise, the couple arrived at the hotel only after wild drinking bouts at the Rendezvous, the Plantation, Club Gallant or a speakeasy."

Mayfield also writes that one time when Scott and Zelda were going to have tea at the Astor they were so drunk they passed each other in the lobby several times without recognizing each other. "A violent, destructive note had crept into Scott's binges," Mayfield says. "Anita Loos braved current stories of his strange behavior to have dinner with the Fitzgeralds at Gateway Drive. Before going to the table she and Zelda waited for Scott until almost time for the servants to leave. Just as the roast was brought on, Scott staggered in. 'You didn't wait for me!' he shrieked. 'Why didn't you?!'"

Fitzgerald had lived in far humbler digs than the Plaza or his estate in Great Neck prior to publishing *This Side of Paradise* and his literary output seemed to suffer accordingly. He lived at 200 Claremont Avenue, which he described as a "high, horrible apartment house in the middle of nowhere (near Columbia University)," Mayfield says, and he failed to sell a single one of the dozen plus stories he wrote there.

Several decades earlier a certain Duke escorted a woman to the Grill room of The Plaza for a late snack. The chef there obligingly whipped up some ultra thin pancakes for desert, then asked the Duke what his friend's name was. "Suzette," replied the Duke. Hence, Crepes Suzette! was born.

"There was one night, the night of the big blizzard of 1948," the late Anna Sosenko, Hildegarde's longtime manager, told me. "Everything was cancelled. She worked for two tables of people. That never fazed Hildegarde. She gave the same performance she always gave."

Of course, under normal weather conditions, most bookings at The Plaza were like a New York Yankees playoff—more than 100 percent sold out.

When The Plaza was built there was a seismic shift of celebrities to the northern fringes of the theater district and The Plaza.

Two of the most frequent celebrity visitors to the Plaza in those early days were James ("Diamond Jim") Brady, the fabulously wealthy railroad contractor, and his voluptuous gal pal actress Lillian Russell. Brady was a prodigious eater. George Rector, the priority of Rectors, once quipped Brady was "the best 25 customers we had." At one sitting he'd eat six or seven lobsters, a huge steak and an assortment of French pastry. But Brady, who was said to have been worth an estimated $12 million, or as much as it cost to build the Plaza in 1907, was not your average rich guy. He wore his wealth on his sleeve quite literally. His collection of gems included more than 20,000 diamonds and, according to one account, when he donned some of them he "looked like an excursion steamer at twilight"— or the living embodiment of a grand hotel.

At 250 pounds, with porcine eyes gazing over his bulldog jaw, Brady was no matinee idol and when he squired attractive if plumpish Russell to the theater or the Palm Court they were dubbed, behind their backs, "beauty and the beast." Brady's great love was a former shop girl named Edna McCauley, who first caught his eye as she strutted in Peacock Alley in the old Waldorf-Astoria at 34th Street and Fifth Avenue. But when Brady's friend Jesse Lewisohn was ill and staying at Brady's farm Brady made the mistake of sending McCauley to help him recover. Lewisohn was soon well enough to sail to Europe—with McCauley.

Lillian Russell, by the way, would wheel her diamond-studded bicycle into the hotel. It was at the time insured for the princely sum of $10,000. I've always wondered whatever happened to it—and can picture it stowed away yet in some back closet at The Plaza.

Decades later, the stars were still coming. The Beatles, for instance, came, stayed, and conquered. And they were just as much real life fun as "Eloise." The super group first came to New York and The Plaza in 1964 when they did "The Ed Sullivan Show" on TV. They stayed in suites 1260, 1263, 1264 and 1273 on the less exclusive 58th Street side of the hotel (without the view of Central Park) "so they wouldn't be as noticeable if they looked out the window," one internal hotel memo noted. Actually, The Beatles were registered under their own names—which is definitely not the case with celebrities today—because few "adults" were aware how popular they had already become with young people. The Plaza was to find out soon enough as thousands lined up from Fifth Avenue to the Pulitzer Fountain to get even one glimpse of the "Fab Four."

For the most part, The Beatles were far better behaved than their fans. I say for the most part because there was one "incident" that was rather scandalous for the times—at least for the hotel. One of the Beatles was being photographed jumping up and down on the bed in his room and you'd think he was trashing it in our modern sense. Publicity manager Eve Brown raced up to the room and said, "Now you stop this nonsense this very minute!" The Plaza, over the years, got more accustomed to celebrities "cutting up."

The next year, the Beatles played at Sheer Stadium. "Their plane landed at the Kennedy airport and taxied to a remote hangar, two miles distant from the waiting throngs at the main terminal and the Beatles were quickly transported by limousine to the Warwick Hotel in Manhattan where they held a press conference. Later that same evening they had a third get-together with Bob Dylan," writes Bill Yenne in his book *The Beatles*.

Their main purpose was to give a concert at Shea Stadium, home of the Mets baseball team. This "marked what may have been the apex of the Beatles' touring career," Yenne continues in his book. Everything about the concert at Shea Stadium was oversized—a theatrical extravaganza of unusually large proportions. It was the largest stadium ever played in by a rock band and, with a capacity of 56,000 held the largest crowd that had ever attended an outdoor concert. Even their arrival at Shea Stadium was pure theater: after being transported by helicopter to the site of the World's Fair (in Flushing Meadows, Queens), which was immediately adjacent to Shea Stadium, they made their entrance (into the stadium arena) by armored car."

Bobby D'Angelo has been at The Plaza in the banquet department since the time the Beatles stayed there. He later became the administrative secretary of the banquet department, booking the waiters and doing a lot of the clerical work. But he'll never forget the Beatles. "At that time they were really new so you didn't know what was going on," he relates. "But you knew it was something that was going to take off. They came in on February 4, 1964 and they stayed about four days. They went to the Ed Sullivan show. I remember that Ringo (Starr) was a comic. He used to kid around. He was the outspoken one. George Harrison was very quiet. Always very quiet. I was a banquet waiter at the time. I served them breakfast in the Baroque Suite, a banquet room—all the way down the end of the hall at the very far west end of the hotel (facing Fifth Avenue on the second floor of The Plaza). They had a lot of publicity people. They had disc jockeys that were here. They were all with them and their publicist. All their entourage. They were nice to serve, though. They were regular people. They weren't demanding or anything …

"Jerry Lewis is very demanding. I met him a couple of times. I really didn't care for him. Electricians here used to tell me he used to call them to bring up a light bulb and he was so nasty to them."

Back to the Beatles. "One night that I worked and served them dinner in a suite overlooking Bethesda Fountain on the Fifth Avenue side and all these kids were outside, all carrying on, yelling and screaming. So my buddy who I was working with combs his hair down on his forehead and then goes back to the window and waves and the kids outside went wild. I said to him, 'Let's get out of here before they come upstairs and attack us here.' There were (only) a couple hundred kids. But the (screaming) was constant. The Beatles were staying in the suite where the King of Morocco has stayed."

At a time when cash deposits were often required the Beatles "had insured their reservations by the simple expedient of using their own names," writes Eve Brown, the former Plaza publicist in her book, *The Plaza*. "Fifteen rooms needed, for six days—representing a nice piece of change even by Plaza standards," she continues. "Plaza patrons and managers shuddered to think what might happen to the rare, original lumiere jardinières in the Palm Court and the priceless crystal girondal hurricane lamps, copies of those on the balustrade of Chantilly Palace outside of Paris...(but) not one would shine his shoes with a towel; there wasn't a single cigarette burn on the rug or upholstery, nothing was broken, nothing swiped, not even an ash tray."

What a contrast to actor Daniel Baldwin's stay at The Plaza nearly 35 years later when he reportedly "trashed" his suite on a binge.

The Beatles stayed at the Warwick Hotel in 1966 after The Plaza politely declined another visit by the "Fab Four." However, John Lennon returned to the hotel in the late 1960's on his own and quite incognito. "I know one of the Beatles, I believe it was John Lennon, stayed at the Plaza for months at a time," Chester Deptula, manager of the Surrey, who worked at The Plaza, told me. "This must have been in the late 1960's. He had a beard then and he was never registered under his name. It was all taken care of. I used to talk to his manager all the time."

When the four young Liverpudlians first checked into The Plaza most of the staff, let alone most of the free world, had no inkling of the tidal wave of adoration that would resurface time and time again wherever the Beatles went, just as it would many years later for celebrities like the late Princess Diana and singer Ricky Martin.

"After a couple of months I realized how famous the Beatles were getting, says Plaza Banquet executive D'Angelo. "I said to myself, 'I wish I had gotten all their autographs. I've seen so many famous people here it's incredible. But I don't like to bother them. Some of the waiters will go over and ask for an autograph. I feel they're out to enjoy themselves. You're getting paid to work there. You shouldn't ask for autographs. Only one time I had to get an autograph from Pavarotti because my wife loves the opera. I've served Tony Bennett, Frank Sinatra. Frank Sinatra was a sport. Not cheap at all. You took care of him and he took care of you. He gave you a $100 bill for pouring him a cup of coffee. And he gave a lot, a whole lot to charity you never knew about. That was class. I respect that."

William H. Carr, a former night city editor of the New York *Post*, and the author of many books including the best-selling *The Duponts of Delaware*, says he went to the hotel during the time the Beatles were there to visit old friend Jan Dupont, who usually stayed in the same suite of rooms at The Plaza every time she was in New York.

"I went to visit her for dinner and I see this crowd and I hadn't realized the Beatles were staying there though there were thousands of people. They had gathered in the Pulitzer Fountain area on the Fifth Avenue side of The Plaza. They were spilling over into Fifth Avenue and the cops were having trouble keeping them out of Fifth Avenue. Just an unbelievable mass of teenagers, and I fought my way through."

On April 30, 2005 The Plaza closed for renovations to 350 of its hotel rooms and conversion of the rest of the rooms in to luxury condominiums. The renovations are expected to last two years with the "new" Plaza opening in 2007 on the 100th anniversary of the world's most famous hotel. It was night. No people were lined up with luggage waiting for taxis. Inside the Central Park South entrance a security guard had already been posted in a chair. But the lights were still shinning inside with the promise of laughter and celebration to come. After all, The Plaza is in its own way that eternal "green light" F. Scott Fitzgerald spoke of in "The Great Gatsby." It beats on, to paraphrase the great American author who loved it so much long ago, "boats against the current, borne back ceaselessly into the past."

Cindy Adams, the greatest and toughest New York newspaper columnist since Walter Winchell—although she has the proverbial heart of gold that Winchell rarely opened—has also had a life-long love affair with the hotel. For her, like millions of others, it is not so much a fairytale castle of a building but memories...of a once unknown world which was opened to them. "The Queen of Thailand always used to stay," Adams told New York Magazine in an article called "The Plaza Lives." "I did a TV interview with her. And I walked in wearing a white-tie silk suit and hat. And she came out wearing a white-tie silk suit and hat..." If the Waldorf-Astoria is "America's gilded dream," as I once wrote, The Plaza is our county's reflection—in books, movies and ourselves.

The funky lobby of the Chelsea Hotel as it looks today. Thomas Wolfe, Dylan Thomas, the artist Christo and more artists and writers lived at the Chelsea than any other hotel in New York and maybe the world. Rooms are reasonable by New York standards. You can even stay in the room that Thomas Wolfe is said to have occupied and written part of one of his novels standing up on top of a refrigerator. Highly disciplined, Wolfe often worked all night throwing numbered pages on the floor. Photo by Mark Kasner.

Eli Wallach, seen here at the Waldorf-Astoria at an American Theatre Wing Tony Awards gals with Sandy Dennis, was devoted to the plays of Tennessee Williams, who lived for a time in The Chelsea Hotel (above) and the Elysee Hotel. Photo by Glyn Lewis.

Seen this close, the Carlyle Hotel is impressive in its Art Deco elegance. Seen from Central Park or just west of Central Park, the Carlyle dominates the Upper East Side skyline in the 70s with its distinct gold-painted topmost tower. Photo by Mark Kasner.

The I.M. Pei-designed Four Seasons Hotel on East 57th Street. Mr. Pei said that in designing the Four Seasons he was inspired partly by the Art Deco twin towers of the Waldorf-Astoria. Yet, generally speaking, the famed architect is not all that enamored with design elements of many New York hotels. Photo by Mark Kasner.

The late Ruby Keeler, who was once married to Al Jolson, loved The Carlyle Hotel (above left). A huge star in early "talkies," Keeler made a big comeback in the early 1970s when this photo was taken playing the lead in a revival of the musical "No, No Nannett" on Broadway. Photo by Glyn Lewis.

The Pierre Hotel has been called an "elongated French chateau" and rightly so.
Photo by Mark Kasner.

Artist-author Ludwig Bemelmans painted the murals in Bemelmans Bar in the Carlyle
Hotel over a period of many months. He negotiated a penthouse suite for his labors until
the murals were complete. His whimsical view of animals and people in Central Park has
delighted both children and adults for several generations. Photo by Mark Kasner.

Another Bemelmans
mural in Bemelmans bar.

Another current shot of the
Chelsea Hotel. It's been 93 years
since first-class passengers who
survived the ordeal at sea after
the Titanic struck an iceberg
were put up at the Chelsea.

The late Zero Mostel, who starred on Broadway in "Fiddler on the Roof," shares a morsel with an unidentified lady at Sardi's Restaurant, which is a favorite of New Yorkers and out-of-towners who come to shows and hotels in the Broadway theater district.
Photo by Glyn Lewis.

The elegant simplicity of its front entrance is in sharp contrast to the magnificance of some of its grand suites overlooking Central Park.

The Ansonia Hotel, a favorite of musicians, especially opera singers, because the walls are so thick and they could practice for the most part without worrying about waking up their neighbors. Serious thought was given to tearing it down, like the Astor before it. Now apartments go for millions as Manhattan's Upper West Side is more desirable for many, especially, writers, actors and other artists, than the more staid Upper East Side. Photo by Mark Kasner.

Actress Celeste Holm, who starred on Broadway in the original prodcuction of "Oklahoma!", enjoys a lighter moment at one New York hotel soiree. Photo by Glyn Lewis.

Actress Maureen O'Sullivan makes a toast at a gala for Broadway's Tony Awards at The Waldorf-Astoria. Photo by Glyn Lewis.

The late silent screen star Lillian Gish lived very comfortably for years on East 57th Street but enjoyed the good life inside New York's grand hotels. Photo by Glyn Lewis.

Actress Debbie Reynolds is all smiles at a party in the grand ballroom of The Waldorf-Astoria. She became a major star co-starring with Gene Kelly in "Singing in the Rain" and is still a big crowd pleaser in casino theaters and other major venues. Photo by Glyn Lewis.

Another shot of the Chelsea Hotel with its roofline and chimneys. Writers Arthur Miller, Thomas Wolfe and Pete Hamill lived here among many other giants in the arts.

When he was staying at The Carlyle Hotel to work on his memoirs, President Harry Truman used to drive his secret service guards crazy by walking briskly up Madison Avenue. "Hey, Harry, how's it going!?" was a common greeting to one of our most approachable and down-to-earth US Presidents. Photo by Mark Kasner.

Unlike the Waldorf-Astoria or The Plaza, with their grand entrances on major avenues, the front entrance of the Carlyle Hotel is on a side street, east 76th Street in Manhattan. But its less audacious entrance is no indication that the level service at the Carlyle is below that of these other top hotels. In fact, many say the Carlyle has the best service in the city. When my son, William Morehouse, stepped into the dining room for breakfast one Saturday morning when he was three years old, he dropped a stick he had found in the park. One of the doormen found us and asked William, "Did you drop your stick, sir?" Photo by Mark Kasner.

The Mark Hotel on East 77th Street is a favorite of movie stars and models, including Isabella Rosselli who told me she doesn't go there as much any more since she moved the Manhattan's West Side.

Dwarfed by the Waldorf-Astoria and its twin towers The Mark nevertheless has its own imposing mini tower on Madison Avenue. I went to nursery school on 78th Street and Madison at the Walt Whitman School, which is no longer there, and don't remember The Mark or the Carlyle but the soda fountain across Madison.

The Lowell Hotel on East 63rd Street near Madison Avenue is the ultimate "boutique hotel" where F. Scott Fitzgerald stayed when he was in New York long after he stayed in and wrote about The Plaza and cavorted with his wife, Zelda, in the Pulitzer Fountain in front of The Plaza.

The late Hume Cronyn lived for years with his wife, the late Jessica Tandy, at the Wyndham Hotel on West 58th Street across from The Plaza. While not as posh as The Lowell (pictured above), The Wyndam had been popular with Hollywood actors, including Ginger Rogers, who loved its oversized rooms and big kitchens. Photo by Glyn Lewis.

[top and bottom] Whoppie Goldberg, Kathie Couric, Oprah and other celebrities like to stay and dine at The Four Seasons. Some celebrities and VIPs like the suites on the north side of the hotel which afford sweeping views of Central Park.

The cavernous lobby of The Four Seasons has an other worldly quality to it or as if it was a scene out of Orson Wells' *Citizen Kane*. Photo by Mark Kasner.

Glamorous actress Dina Merrill, the consumate Boadway and Hollywood star, is also a socialite who is much sought after to attend major charity dinners and galas in New York City hotels. Photo by Glyn Lewis.

A boyish-looking Michael Caine, long before he costarred in the film "Dirty Rotten Scoundrels" with Steve Martin, enjoys a pensive moment in a New York hotel restaurant.
Photo by Glyn Lewis.

Artist Marc Chagall (r) looks up at Martin Riskin, who held executive positions at The Plaza, The Pierre and The Waldorf-Astoria.

This brass plaque pays homage to Thomas Wolfe, who along with Dylan Thomas, are the only two authors so honored at the entrance to the Chelsea Hotel. Photo by Mark Kasner.

Bruno Tison, executive chef of The Plaza for many years, has had to look for work elsewhere after The Plaza closed April 30, 2005, to turn much of the historic hotel into cooperative apartments. Tison personally looked after Mick Jagger of Rolling Stones fame when Jagger celebrated his 50th birthday party at The Plaza.

The twin towers of The Waldorf-Astoria soar several stories above the hotel's top-most 42nd floor, 11 floors above the 33rd floor where the late composer Cole Porter lived for many years and wrote some of the scores for some of his most famous movies and Broadway shows. In the early days of the hotel the towers were rigged with radio antennas for live broadcasts from the hotel's Starlight Roof and Grand Ballroom.

The author of this book slaving away at a manuscript of another book in one of the many suites in The Waldorf-Astoria. Few, if any, New York hotels have the number of multiple room suites which The Waldorf-Astoria has in profusion. Jerry Lewis, the late Frank Sinatra and many other celebrities have been at home in these costly grand aeries.

The author, his son, William Ward Morehouse and wife, Liz Morehouse, celebrating New Year's Eve 2004 for a night at The Plaza. "A Night at the Plaza" was the name of an original musical I wrote with composer/lyricist David Romeo writing the music and lyrics. The title has been changed to "A Night at the Astor."

Restaurateur George Lang chatting with the author at Lang's 80th birthday at Hotel Des Artists. Lang owns the extraordinarilysuccessful Cafe Des Artists in the West 67th Street "hotel" which retains its original name but has mostly permanent residents, some of whom have paid millions for their apartments.. Legend has it that artist Howard Chandler Christie used to trade art work for meals. Now, some of Christie's paintings of scantily clad women fetch upwards of $1 million each.

My stepmother, Rebecca Morehouse (r), who lived at The Plaza with my father, the late New York drama critic Ward Morehouse, for 11 years. With her at the now defunct Stork Club is the late Ethel Barrymore, John and Lionel Barrymore's sister. Ethel's success in the theater was both early and long. John was a leading man on Broadway, in silent films and early talkies. Lionel had some of his greatest success as an older character actor long after John had died.

Pianist/singer extraordinaire Kathleen Landis has been a fixture at the Cafe Pierre in the Pierre Hotel for years. She's befriended many of the regulars who drink and dine there as well as permanent hotel residents such as Roy Neuberger, the financier and fabulous art collector.

Billionaire Donald Trump, now star of "The Apprentice" on TV, with his then wife, Ivana Trump, in 1991 with Trump bestowing the "Jerusalem Founders Man of the Year Award" on Lawrence Harvey, the Plaza Hotel's director of Catering. Trump wooed Harvey to The Plaza from The Waldorf-Astoria. (Photo courtesy of the Lawrence Harvey collection.)

Cafe Pierre's Kathleen Landis taking a much deserved break from her fabulous renditions of George Gershwin and Cole Porter. Landis is as nice as she is talented, offers other singers a chance in the spotlight, including rising pop/rock singer EJ.

The author flanked by Texas oil heiress and hotel baroness Caroline Hunt and Erin Jo (r) Jurow, widow of the late Hollywood producer Martin Jurow, who produced film "Breakfast at Tiffany's" with Audrey Hepburn. Hepburn was a frequent guest at the Carlyle Hotel which has been managed by Hunt's Rosewood Corporation, which also runs the famed Mansion Hotel in Dallas where this photo was taken.

A surprise party circa 1910 at the Hotel Ansonia for the children of guests at the hotel. This was an era of the hotel—and hotels in New York in general—when entire families lived in hotels for months if not years at a time. Opera great Enrico Caruso lived at the Ansonia for a time but there is no record of him charging a hotel clock with a kitchen knife as he reportedly did at The Plaza when its buzzing sound disturbed him. (Photo courtesy of the Museum of the City of New York.)

The author's father, columnist and critic Ward Morehouse, with his mother Joan Marlowe Rahe, a former Broadway actress and publisher, with actress Jane Wyman, who was Ronald Reagan's first wife and an unidentified man. This photo was taken in 1941 in Hawaii several months before the Japanese attacked Pearl Harbor. My mother and father lived at The Plaza in New York from 1944-1945 and later at The Waldorf-Astoria.

In 1900, trolleys whizzed by the first Grand Central Station on 42nd Street. The building in back of the old Grand Central is the Manhattan Hotel, which looked remarkably like the Plaza Hotel, which opened several years later in 1907. The Manhattan was raised to make way for an office building. Both the Plaza and Manhattan were designed by Henry J. Hardenberg. (Photo courtesy of the collection of Lorraine Diehl.)

The Astor Hotel had roof garden dining areas just as many other hotels did after the turn of the last century. Even the smaller Algonquin Hotel once featured dining on its considerably smaller roof. Big bands played on another section of the Astor roof and this photograph, taken in 1931, depicts diners living in an era, albeit in the early years of the Great Depression, dressed elegantly for lunch. (Photo courtesy of the Museum of the City of New York.)

This is the main dining room of the Algonquin Hotel as it looks today, not having changed much from the heydays of the famed "Algonquin Round Table" in the 1920s. The Round Table was an informal lunch group of columnists, playwrights and assorted wits which once included New York Times Theater Critic Alexander Woollcott. Members of the Roundtable are depicted in the artist's rendering in this photo. Photo by Craig Rosenthal.

Once it started, construction was rapid on The Plaza, opening on October 1, 1907. The first Alfred Vanderbilt was the first to sign the hotel's guest register. "The original marketing plan of the hotel was to attract people like my grandfather," Alfred G. Vanderbilt III told New York Magazine in a May 2005 commemorative article called "The Plaza Lives." Architect Frank Lloyd Wright lived in a suite with one of these rounded rooms when the Guggenheim Museum, which he designed, was being constructed 30 blocks north of The Plaza at 89th Street.

This photo was taken on 3/19/06 shortly after construction began on The Plaza, which sprouted from an area that was dominated by rowhouses but also the Vanlderbilt Mansion just to the South at 57th Street and Fifth Avenue.

King Hussein of Morroco and his grandchildren in the lobby of the Plaza Hotel in 1991. Richard Wilhelm, former President and CEO of The Plaza is on his right. Delegations of royals had been commonplace at the Plaza. But the Plaza said no to one royal who wanted to connect all the rooms and suites on one floor.

[top] Film star Catherine Deneauve with Lawrence Harvey, director of catering for the Plaza Hotel. Deneauve was a frequent guest of big parties at the hotel.

[bottom]
Kwek Leng Beng, Chairman of the Hong Leong Group, parent of CDL Hotels, which owned The Plaza and still owns The Broadway Millennium and Hudson Theatre, the second oldest theater on Broadway. Chairman Kwek has restored the theater to its original 1903 grandeur, which was lost when it became home of "The Tonight Show" with Steve Allen in the 1950s and later "The Jack Paar Show."

John Barrymore (right) in a Broadway drawing room comedy just after the turn of the last century. "The great profile," as Barrymore, the grandfather of film star Drew Barrymore, was called in his day, loved living at The Algonquin.

Prince Alwaleed Bin Talal of Saudi Arabia became co-owner of The Plaza in 1995 before selling it with partner Chairman Kwek nine years later.

The towers of the new Time Warner Center on Central Park West at 59th Street loom over Central Park. The middle portion of the twin glass towers are occupied by the Mandaran Oriental Hotel, which starts on the 35th floor, affording a beautiful view of the park and the city. The top-most floors of the towers are residences. Photo by George Farquhar.

The Plaza Hotel, which opened in 1907, stands on the site of the first Plaza Hotel, which opened in 1891. The Plaza closed in the Spring of 2005 so that many of its rooms can be turned into apartments with kitchens. Ironically, when the hotel first opened most of those who checked in during the first several years became "permanents," guests who lived there for months and even years. And some of them had well-equipped kitchens.

[top] Just to the left of The Plaza Hotel is Trump Tower where billionaire Donald Trump calls home. The building with the spire is the Sherry Netherland, where the late Lucille Lortel, the so-called "Queen of Off-Broadway," lived in a big apartment complete with terrace after she left The Plaza, where she also lived for some years. Photo by George Farquhar.

[bottom] Pierre Hotel at 61st and Fifth Avenue. The "shadow" is the shadow of the Sherry-Netherland Hotel, its immediate neighbor to the south. Photo by George Farquhar.

[top] Street Lamp in Central park and Essex House. A number of years ago when the hotel was less cared for the first three letter of "Essex" went out and ..."SEX HOUSE" is all that could be seen at night. Now a distinctive Starwood property, that kind of thing doesn't happen anymore. Photo by George Farquhar.

[bottom] Central Park looks a lot like it did when Diamond Jim Brady lived at The Plaza in the early part of the last century. But it took Donald Trump to rebuild the skating rink in the park after others took too long to renovate it. Photo by George Farquhar.

CHAPTER 8
THE ROARING OF THE ROARING TWENTIES

By the 1920's Jazz age midtown Manhattan hotels had become the playground for the brightest stars of the age.

Like they were at the turn of the century, 1920's hotels were playgrounds for show business people. Though down from its historic highs of the 1920's when in 1928 nearly 300 shows opened on Broadway, the Broadway theater of 1939 was booming. In fact, there were 17 members of the Critics' Circle in 1939—which also hints at how many daily newspapers there were in those days. There were actually nine, not counting *PM*.

William Randolph Hearst built the Warwick Hotel in 1927 for his mistress, actress Marion Davies. Almost at the exact time Hearst and his glamorous paramour danced under the stars on the terraces of their penthouse, Mrs. Hearst was playing poker with Elsa Maxwell in her Waldorf Towers apartment and fuming about "that bitch," according to my stepmother, legendary Broadway producer Jean Dalrymple who was also playing cards at the Waldorf. Yet despite its formerly spectacular views of Central Park, the noise at the Warwick from the old Sixth Avenue El, even from Miss Davies' expensive perch, drove the mostly even-tempered Miss Davies to beg the Lord of San Simeon to build her a private house on quieter East 64th Street near Fifth.

The Warwick Hotel was also the scene of the free-fall of F. Scott Fitzgerald, which Budd Schulberg documents in his book, *The Disenchanted*. After working on some of the dialogue for *Gone with the Wind*, Fitzgerald was sent east with the much younger Schulberg to research a movie called *Winter Carnival*. When Schulberg took a break to see some New York friends, Fitzgerald went AWOL to a local dive, leaving a note which said ominously, "You shouldn't have left me Pal."

115

Aaron Latham, in his book, *Crazy Sundays: F. Scott Fitzgerald in Holly-wood*, recounts that, "The younger man brought the older one back to the hotel and put him through the treatment: black coffees, cold showers. Fitzgerald sobered up enough to apologize and then Schulberg apologized, too. They promised each other to work, *work*, and the rest of the night they tried to. After all, they had a deadline. That morning they were supposed to report to Wanger's suite and tell him their Carnival story."

The Croydon Hotel, built in 1923, was the home of Harold Arlen, who wrote the music for *The Wizard of Oz*. Located on East 86th Street between Fifth and Madison Avenues, Anthony Quinn and Henry Fonda also lived there for a time. Just west of the Croydon was The Adams, which like The Croydon, has been converted into an apartment house. The Adams was where the John Guare film *Six Degrees of Separation* was partially shot and Alexander R. Raydon, the director of Raydon Gallery at 1091 Madison Avenue, just a few blocks to the South, remembers supplying art for the scenes of the movie that were shot at The Adams. Both the Croydon and The Adams were more "apartment hotels," with some services like The Plaza or Waldorf-Astoria.

I will call these and many other hotels built in the 1920's the calm before the storm, the quiet more residential palaces which went up before the last gasp of the jazz age vaulted into the Art Deco and architectural heavens of The Waldorf-Astoria, Hampshire House, Pierre, Carlyle and even the old Emery Roth-designed St. Moritz, all completed before 1932. These, for the most part, were skyscrapers with all the amenities of a country home—in size of their apartments, and even in the views of the heavens they afforded guests in places like Waldorf-Astoria's Starlight Roof open to the night sky.

In the 1920s even up to the 1940s and beyond some of the finest buildings along Central Park West, for instance, were really glorified residential hotels. These include the Beresford at 81st Street and the Aden, on block north. Even the Dakota at 72nd Street had a full-service kitchen for its residents. "We would order things from the kitchen when we lived there at the Dakota for the first time," Erin Jo Jurow, the widow of Martin Jurow, who produced the films *Breakfast at Tiffany's* and the original *Pink Panther*, told me.

Residential hotels like the Drake, The Lombardy and the Warwick provided "freedom from drudgery, the servant problem, plus the many responsibilities that go with maintaining large private homes," a news account of the day explained. And what these more sedate looking structures lacked in architectural flamboyance they made up for with their flamboyant guests.

The Mayflower Hotel, built in the 1920s on Central Park West at 61st Street, was also an apartment hotel for those who stayed there for extended periods of time. It offered big, spacious suites with walk-in closets which weren't as expensive as some of the luxury hotels and it was just enough off the beaten track to afford stars and celebrities the privacy they couldn't get on the other side of Central Park. Moreover, a lot of actors liked it because they weren't bothered as much by tourists.

Before Robert DeNiro moved to Tribeca he lived at the Mayflower in the 1980s for a few years. He was private. It was sort of understood, a former manager of the hotel told me. Joe Pesci, who was a close friend of Mr. DeNiro's, also lived there. Mr. Pesci was just the opposite; he was one of the guys. He used to hang out with hotel employees and even get them coffee on occasion. Robert Duvall and singer Roy Orbison stayed at the Mayflower as did John Houseman, whenever he was in New York. Mickey Rooney stayed there for a while when he was in *Sugar Babies* on Broadway but he wanted a more lively place. Houseman, who was in the TV series "The Paper Chase" at the time, looked so much like the character he played on TV, a professor Kingsfield, that one of the front desk employees had the audacity to address him as "Professor Kingsfield, I Presume." Houseman, who had a reputation for being aloof off camera and off stage, smiled when the front desk clerk addressed him by his alter ego.

In an effort to avoid what they feared would be landmark status, the hotel stripped off its gorgeous terra cotta skin and replaced it with a sandstone-colored cement-like mixture. An article in *The New York Times* at the time called this the "deflowering of the Mayflower."

One thing that never changed until recent years at The Mayflower was a bell captain named "Whitey." He knew every configuration of every room and would sometimes intervene with the front desk if he felt this or that guest would be happier in another suite in the hotel.

Ann Miller stayed at the Mayflower for a number of months when she was in *Sugar Babies* with Rooney. She had a grinding schedule, performing eight times a week and coming home late in the evening. She'd run the water to take a hot bath but she would fall not only asleep but deep asleep and the tub would fill up and her entire suite would be flooded, so bad that it would cascade ("like Niagara Falls," one source said) to the floor below. It happened at least three times. She'd call down to the front desk and a night manager ran upstairs to her suite with a bellman and Ms. Miller would be there on the bed. She didn't dare get off the bed because the apartment had so much water in it.

"What am I going to do?! What am I going to do?!" the frantic Ms. Miller yelled to the bellman. He told her to calm down and virtually carried her to the safety of the corridor. But because of who Ms. Miller was the hotel cleaned up her apartment and apologized to the guests as far as four floors below her.

Another incident at the Mayflower caused much more of a stir. The Chieftains, a group of Irish singers, used to stay at the hotel every year around St. Patrick's Day. And one night very late they arrived at the hotel very drunk and they got stuck on the elevator around the fifth floor. Now they caused even more of a ruckus, waking up a number of the guests in the hotel. Finally, the manager on duty had to call the fire department. When the firemen arrived they were going to use their axes to break down the ornate old elevator door but when the night manager called the general manager, who lived in the hotel, to tell them what they were going to do, he said, "If the firemen touch that door you're fired!" As the Chieftain's manager arrived, he added to the crescendo of screams already coming from the trapped elevator. The night manager then, fearing for his job, literally placed himself in front of the door and was ready to be handcuffed by police when a man from the elevator company showed up just in the nick of time. He got the door open and the Chieftains were quietly put in their room and allowed to sleep it off.

The fabulous West End and Broadway star Tallulah Bankhead lived at the Elysee Hotel on East 54th Street until she moved into a townhouse on East 62nd Street. After jauntily stepping off the *Aquitania* on January 13, 1931, "Tallulah went directly to the Elysee Hotel (a big advertiser in *Theater* magazine) on East Fifty-fourth Street, off Park Avenue," writes Lee Israel in her biography *Miss Tallulah Bankhead*. She moved into a spacious and elegant twelfth-floor suite whose previous tenant had been Ethel Barrymore. The sofas and chairs were done in modest chintz; there were inlaid commodes and smoking tables. The grand piano was covered with a rich Chinese embroidery.

"The staff of the Elysee, alerted to Tallulah's distinguished international reputation, were especially solicitous when they discovered that a call for ice, or bootleg liquor, or a pair of nylons was likely to bring a $20 tip. Tallulah kept them hopping but they hopped eagerly."

Miss Bankhead later sometimes stayed at the posher Gotham Hotel on West 55th Street across Fifth Avenue from Mr. Astor's pride and joy, the St. Regis, most notably when she was seeking the part of Scarlet O'Hara in David O. Selznick's film version of Margaret Mitchell's novel *Gone with the Wind*.

"I have many excellent movie offers but as you have probably heard I may do *Gone with the Wind*," she wrote a friend while staying at the Gotham, according to Ms. Israel's book. "I am the top candidate. Say nothing but pray for your little girl."

Bankhead was married to John Barrymore look-a-like John Emery and was living in her enormous suite at the Gotham when she starred in her now infamous production of Shakespeare's *Antony and Cleopatra*. While some critics were kind and actually liked a lot of her acting in the play, John Mason Brown (and not Dorothy Parker as is usually assumed) wrote that "Tallulah Bankhead barged down the Nile last night as Cleopatra—and sank."

When her funds dried up temporarily she and Emery had to move out of the Gotham and later moved back to the more reasonably-priced Gramercy Park Hotel, which she always called her favorite hotel.

The Gramercy Park Hotel, on the northern fringe of Gramercy Park, the city's only private park, has a history as colorful as its guests or its history is its colorful guests. Currently it serves as the home of several noted writers, including Ira Gasman, who wrote the book and lyrics for the Broadway musical *The Life*. Eleven-year-old John F. Kennedy lived at the hotel with parents Rose and Joseph P. Kennedy at one time. Humphrey Bogart married Helen Menchen on the hotel's roof garden when he was a young leading man on Broadway, when he uttered his now famous line, "Tennis, anyone?" It was to be several years before he would repeat his performance in *The Petrified Forrest* on Broadway in the movies and become an international film star. Babe Ruth reportedly got so loud and belligerent at the bar—more recently a favorite haunt of Peter O'Toole, Sting and Matt Dillon—that he was asked to leave.

"After the First World War with the decline in luxury town house construction and the demise of notable entertainment palaces such as Delmonico's, the great hotels took on an increased significance. In the minds of the general public hotels carried the main burden of social and aesthetic trend setting," Robert A.M. Stern, Gregory Gilmartin and Thomas Mellins write in *New York 1930*.

It's interesting to note that newspapers of the day even carried hotel columns. "At the Hotels," was a column in *The New York Times* which carried news of the comings and goings of guests, something which would be unheard of today for security reasons alone.

Beginning with Prohibition, however, speakeasies, the authors of *New York 1900* say, took the place of some favorite hotel watering holes. The Knickerbocker, as has been mentioned earlier, was turned into an office building in 1921, only 15 years after it opened. Yet several notable hotels, including the 500-room Ambassador, built in 1921 on Park Avenue between 51st and 52nd Streets, a block north of St. Bartholomew Church, and the 1100-room Roosevelt, which came along in 1924, occupying an entire city block (the only other hotel besides the Waldorf to do that) from Madison to Vanderbilt from 46th Street to 47th Streets, were cropping up. The Roosevelt was built with shops opening on the entire ground floor, following the lead of the Astor on 44th Street and Broadway and nearby Biltmore. By contrast, the Ambassador's smaller lobby, was reminiscent of those in neighboring Park Avenue houses to the North.

Long after Herald Square ceased to function as the city's theatrical mecca, the 43-story New Yorker, with a whopping 2,503 rooms, rose near Pennsylvania Station at 34th Street and Eight Avenue.

The great Russian born actress Nazimova, who took Broadway by storm in the early part of the 20th century with her emotionally and sexually charged versions of classics, went on to briefly become one of the highest paid stars in silent films before she became even more famous for her "Garden of Allah" bungalow compound built around her Sunset Boulevard mansion. It was the Bel Air of its day. In New York City, she lived at the old Buckingham Hotel on West 57th Street. (The Garden of Allah opened in 1926.) In her later years, she spent an increasing amount of time writing her memoirs, which were never published. Besides Nazimova, the Buckingham has had a long association with concert pianists of the highest caliber. There is a Paderewski room where the late Ignacy Paderewski lived. Others included Bobby Vaan, Giovanna Martinelli and Galo Barieri.

One of the most unusual real estate hotel deals of the 1920's was The Emery Roth-designed Ritz Tower, completed in 1926. At 13, Roth came to America from Czechoslovakia in search of an uncle in Chicago. But he didn't even have his address and, a year later, went to work as an office boy in an architectural firm. In 1893 he came to New York to join a firm headed by Richard M. Hunt, whose business was largely designing mansions. Roth designed the Ritz Tower at 57th Street and Park Avenue, the Mayflower Hotel, the Drake, St. Moritz and many, many others. He also lived in a residential hotel, the Alden on Central Park West, where he died. In addition to The Ritz Tower he designed The Oliver Cromwell Hotel at 12 West 72nd Street, The Eldorado Apartments at 800 Central Park West and St. Moritz (now The Ritz-Carlton) 500 Central Park South.

The Ritz Tower was the brainchild of Hearst columnist Arthur Brisbane as part of newspaper czar William Randolph Hearst's extensive 1920's New York real estate empire, an empire which crumbled in the Great Depression. Under an agreement with a Ritz-Carlton Hotel executive, The Ritz Tower was operated as an apartment hotel.

Most of the apartments from floor 3 to 18 had two to three rooms and serving pantries. There were a number of duplexes, one of the largest of which Brisbane reserved for himself.

William Randolph Hearst's Warwick Hotel and Ritz Tower were only two of the newspaper baron's many Manhattan real estate holdings, which together were valued, according to contemporary accounts, at between $30 and $40 million. But when the bottom fell out of the market in the Depression, Hearst panicked and divested himself of many of these properties. Had he not, his heirs might have had New York real estate valued at many times that of what, say, the Durst family assembled in Times Square. Nevertheless, some of Hearst's flamboyant lifestyle rubbed off on his chief New York editor, Arthur Brisbane, who also headed up his real estate interests. In the Ritz Tower, for example, Brisbane's duplex apartment on the 18th and 19th floors boasted a living room that was 62 feet long and 30 feet wide with a 24 foot high ceiling. By contrast, Lucius Boomer, who built The new Waldorf-Astoria in 1931 had a big living room but it was just 40 feet long.

The Sherry-Netherland, another castle-like building, has been the home of many celebrities since it was built in the 1920's. Charles Barrett, a top Hollywood and TV publicist for many years, set up many interviews in hotels for stars promoting movies and series. "When I worked at 20th Century Fox in New York on the *French Connection* opening, one of the actors was staying at the Sherry-Netherland Hotel."

"He apparently had a fondness for silver plated teapots, nice hotel china (cups, saucers) and when he was checking out he apparently decided to place a number of these items in a bag he had, according to a publicist who was with him at the time (not me). The bellman came and took the bags away downstairs and when they arrived in the lobby—the bag with all the goodies opened up and out fell the tea pot. When he got downstairs to check out he was aghast, I was told. He then proceeded to tell them the bag was his niece's who had left for Paris and that she was a very naughty young lady for doing such a thing and that he would tell her father. He was beet red. The desk manager and the bellman later told the publicist that the bag had his name on it and that it was not really necessary to steal from the hotel…if he liked the items he could have paid for them, they said. Needless to say the actor never stayed there again, I heard, but rather asked for a room at The Plaza."

Marty Kaufman, a co-producer of *Grand Hotel* on Broadway, maintained an Art Deco masterpiece of an apartment at the Sherry-Netherland. It overlooked The Plaza and could have been the stage set for a Noël Coward play. The Queen of Off-Broadway, Lucille Lortel, also lived here after being at The Plaza for many years. I interviewed her several times at the Sherry-Netherland.

To commemorate its 75th anniversary in 2001, the Hotel Inter-Continental New York was renamed the Inter-Continental The Barclay New York to reclaim its original Barclay name. Inter-Continental The Barclay New York was known familiarly as The Barclay and opened in November 1926. President Clinton used The Barclay as his New York headquarters during his 1992 Presidential Campaign. Modern day stars like Whitney Houston and Gloria Estefan have stayed at the hotel as well as Bette Davis, Marlon Brando, Gloria Swanson, Mary Pickford, Marlon Brando, Jimmie Durante, Debbie Reynolds, Ernest Hemingway and David O. Selznick. Harold Stirling Vanderbilt lived at the hotel for 16 years. The inventor of the card game contract bridge, he had his own squash court and gymnasium at the hotel. It has also served as the official New York residence of Miss America since 1958. The hotel's 686 guest rooms, including 86 suites, were renovated in 1978 at a cost of $32 million and have since had a multimillion dollar rejuvenation.

Cross & Cross, the builders that erected The Barclay in 1926, also built Tiffany & Co. According to a promotion at the time, The Barclay had a separate children's dining room because "little folk need to be released from the formality of a hotel dining room…so it has provided a charming room for them and their nurses." At the same time, when Frank Costello dined at the hotel six men would stand guard. Just west of The

Barclay Hotel was the Park Lane, built in 1924 between 48th and 49th just east of Park Avenue and just west of "Park Lane," which ran through the middle of the block separating The Barclay and the Park Lane. Suites in both hotels were generally leased on a yearly basis and included daily maid service, access to room service and other traditional hotel amenities.

A young Elvis Presley also stayed at the Warwick. Among the letters Elvis got at the Warwick c/o the Warwick Hotel was one from friends Oscar Davis and Tom Diskin.

> "Dear Elvis,
>   Congratulations on a wonderful job. We think you turned in a real sensational performance. Best to you and the Colonel."

At the Stanhope, composer/producer Quincy Jones has conducted his international music business from the comfort of a plush couch angled in the corner of a large suite nearest the front entrance of the Metropolitan Museum of Art. Tina Turner requests the same suite—when Jones isn't there, that is. Ex-Beatle Paul McCartney and his wife Linda stayed a few floors above this as did Charlton Heston, but "way in the back," according to longtime employees. McCartney, riding a new wave of success as a classical composer, has confided that he's had a difficult time getting out from behind the revered ghost of the late John Lennon, who was murdered just across Central Park at the Dakota. Memories are still vivid at the hotel of the time movie star tough guy and art collector extraordinaire Edward G. Robinson was mugged out front on the corner of Fifth Avenue and 81st Street; one of the doormen saved him from harm. Things didn't work out so quickly when another doorman lost Robinson's little dog in Central Park and it took nearly half the Central Park police precinct several hours before the dog was found safe and sound.

The Stanhope is the professional home of entertainer Steve Ross, who got his big break at the Algonquin several decades earlier. Ross, who *New York Times* critic Stephan Holden said, "looks like he was born in a Tuxedo," plays the piano and sings at The Stanhope restaurant.

Guy Lombardo was doing his thing at the 1013-room Roosevelt, which in recent years has had extensive renovation, long before "Mr. New Year's Eve" became synonymous with New Year's Eve in the grand ballroom of the Waldorf-Astoria. When I stayed at the Roosevelt during the research on this book I felt there was a distinct grandmotherly feeling to the hotel. It was like going back in time to when my grandparents used to stay in New York City hotels in a one-bedroom suite and take us to dinner in cavernous dining rooms downstairs. I believe one time they stayed at the then Statler on 55th Street which is now the Park Central. Going downstairs to dinner it was almost like I was going to my grandmother's native Ithaca, New York, instead of a hotel dining room like Astoria.

So, too, some who have spent their honeymoon at the Roosevelt have their own associations with the past. "Some of the people who come back to the hotel have the original copies of bills for their honeymoon and we honor it—give them a room for the original price," Rose Garofalo, a salesman at the hotel, told me during a tour of the Terrace Room where Guy Lombardo once played.

But almost all of the above mentioned establishments are a far cry from the elegance of a hotel built just seven years after the Roosevelt. A hotel named The Pierre.

CHAPTER 9

THE PIERRE

The outrageous incident took place 4:00 a.m., three days after New Year's Eve in 1972, and it might have been right out of a Fred Astaire-Ginger Rogers movie except that it was the most publicized robbery in New York hotel history. Elegantly attired gentlemen bandits, in tuxedos and patent leather shoes, tied up 21 employees, ransacked 47 safe-deposit boxes and sped off in a waiting limousine. To this day, the robbery, which officials at the time estimated to be valued at $4 million, remains unsolved. The Pierre does strive to accommodate every guest, but those gents took that notion of hospitality too far!

If the Plaza is New York's ultimate architectural wedding cake, The Pierre is its jewel box. From the windows of my Escoffier Suite, during my last stay there, I gazed up Madison Avenue to The Carlyle and remember musing to myself, "It doesn't get any better than this. The Carlyle in the distance. Is that the Lotus Club on East 63rd Street?"

Having ordered room service, I learned that our waiter, Mr. Rodriguez, used to wait on John Wayne when he stayed at the hotel. Today, the 42-story Pierre has 76 co-ops and some 200 transient rooms and suites. Rough and tumble John Wayne used to love to stay there and every time he did he'd ask for "Little Ralphie" to be his room service waiter.

The corner where The Pierre sits at Fifth Avenue and 61st Street, the site of the now-razed Gerry mansion, has ties to the Declaration of Independence. On February 2, 1929, work began to raze the house of Commodore Eldridge T. Gerry, a noted philanthropist, lawyer, and grandson of one of the signers of the Declaration of Independence.

125

Commodore Elbridge Thomas Gerry, 1837-1927, was a reformer. A legal advisor to the American Society for the Prevention of Cruelty to Animals, he also led the movement to found (1875), with the help of Henry Bergh, the New York Society for the Prevention of Cruelty to Children (sometimes called the Gerry Society). He devoted most of his life to this cause, which became national in scope. He and his wife, Louisa M. Gerry had two sons named after wealthy New Yorkers, Peter Goelet and Robert Livingston, and two daughters, Angelica and Francis.

Today, Eldridge T. Gerry, III is the Secretary of the agency his namesake founded. Other family members also sit on the board.

The New York Times first announced "Pierre Hotel to rise on Gerry Home site, $15-million building of 41 stories to replace mansion at Fifth Avenue and 61st Street. Building to have club atmosphere." The Hotel was a joint venture between Charles Pierre Casalasco of Corsica and Wall Street investors, including Otto Kahn, E.F. Hutton and Walter P. Chrysler. Architects Schultz and Weaver patterned the hotel after a French château.

Casalasco had started his career in the hotel industry as a page boy in his father's hotel in Monte Carlo. In New York, Pierre had worked at the famed Louis Sherry restaurant on Fifth Avenue and 44th Street.

On October 1, 1931, when the hotel opened its 700 rooms for business, Casalasco promised "to create an atmosphere of a private club or residence instead of the average hotel atmosphere." Eighty-five-year-old Auguste Escoffier, the so-called "father of French chefs," served as guest chef for the formal gala opening two weeks later. But less than two years later the devastating effects of the Great Depression caused Charles Pierre Casalasco to file for bankruptcy and he died the following year of what some friends and contemporaries thought was a broken heart. Though one critic had at the time called his new hotel "one of the most majestic structures in all New York," Casalasco after the Depression felt only cause for lament: "It will take years to discover whether Society will find itself again. Society no longer exists. Today, it's 'How much money have you?' Yesterday, it was, 'Who are you?'"

But it wasn't long before big bands and tea dances helped The Pierre put itself on a sounder financial footing after a reorganization ploy was adopted. Still battered by heavy debt, The Pierre was purchased by Standard Oil tycoon John Paul Getty in 1938 at a fifth of its nominal value. Twenty years later, seizing on the cooperative bonanza, Getty turned it into a super co-op, with its permanent residents taking ownership of the building. They, in turn lease many of the rooms and suites which don't have Central Park views to transients. Until 2005, the sleek hotel was run by Four Seasons Hotels and Resorts, which manages some 50 properties in 22 countries. Four Seasons had a 21-year management contract. It renovated many of the Pierre's rooms and redesigned the Café Pierre, where singer Kathleen Landis has been playing the piano and singing for 16 years.

"It has often been said that The Rotunda is the signature room of The Pierre." A Pierre press release notes. "The Rotunda's famous *trompe l'oeil* murals are a frequent topic of conversation for guests while they enjoy breakfast, traditional Afternoon Tea, cocktails, canapés or desserts. The Rotunda is truly an urban retreat, with its faux white-marble staircase, domed ceiling, floor-to-ceiling murals and ornate light fixtures. The room itself is reminiscent of old-world charm and even a touch of royalty—a splendid environment for a soothing pause in the day, a time for relaxing with friends, or meeting with business associates. Tables and chairs or love seats, arranged in small, private clusters, make conversing easy and comfortable. The ambience is delightfully peaceful.

"The Rotunda's famous *trompe l'oeil* murals are the work of American artist Edward Melcarth (born 1914, died 1973) in 1967," the release goes on to explain. "It was Mr. Melcarth's intention to bring the style and spirit of the Renaissance paintings into the present. Hence, classic mythological figures like Neptune and Venus are intermingled with a woman who resembles Jacqueline Kennedy Onassis, with her young children, as well as a man in a Nehru jacket, a clothing style popular in the 1960's. Other mythological figures, such as the River Gods and Minerva, share space with a young Adam (posed for by the young model/actor Erik Estrada) and Eve, and the painter's cat, Sasha. Several of the figures were modeled on people from New York society and some of the artist's patrons and benefactors. The sculpted male and female heads above the entrances to The Rotunda and the Café Pierre, as well as the mythological masks above the two entrances, are also the work of the artist."

By contrast, the grand ballroom of The Pierre seats 800 and occupies 8,526 square feet. Even the smaller Cotillion Room, where a scene from *Scent of a Woman*, starring Al Pacino, was shot, seats 350 people comfortably.

Financier Roy Neuberger, who celebrated his 100th birthday in 2003, and lived at The Pierre Hotel since the early 1990s, often quipped that while "he sold stock, he collected art." He started collecting early in his

Wall Street career and by 1967 he received an anonymous bid for his collection worth $6 million. He turned it down and later found out the bid came from Nelson Rockefeller, who also had a huge private collection. Some of the works he owned by Milton Avery, Edward Hopper and others, which went on to be valued in the hundreds of millions of dollars, were hung on the walls of his Pierre suite, much the same as the late Nathan Cummings festooned his suite in the Waldorf Towers with valuable original art works.

It has become a time honored New Year's Eve custom for some select acquaintances to pay a pre-midnight intermission visit to Roy Neuberger at his Pierre residence. The fireworks exploding high above Central Park and the gold glow of the Plaza Hotel fill his cozy library where glasses are lifted.

For New Year's Eve 2003, Kitty Carlisle Hart and her musical director David Lewis joined Mr. Neuberger and his charming grandson, Matthew London, for the occasion. "Upon entering, I went to the Steinway in the dimly lit living room and began singing 'Auld Lang Syne,'" recounts Kathleen Landis. "Surprised, they joined in and we toasted life. I invited Kitty and David to stop down on their way out to hear my quartet in the Café.

"Later, we were coming to the end of our last set of the evening, the dance floor was still filled when a stunning Kitty Carlisle Hart appeared at the top of the stairs. As she and her accompanist, David Lewis, came toward the piano to say goodnight."

Ms. Landis asked Kitty if she would honor them with a song. At first she shook her head no, but the audience, as they recognized her presence, began applauding and she smiled a "yes." Kitty began singing, "I'll Be Loving You, Always." After one chorus they stopped and with her charismatic charm, she asked the room if they'd join her in one more chorus to celebrate the New Year. The festive, noisy room quieted to a hush and from service bar, to bar stool, tables to dance floor, the room became unified in spirit and in three part harmony singing, "Not for just an hour, not for just a day, not for just a year."

While packing up the music and microphones, Ms. Landis exchanged goodnights with a couple on their way out. She, still wearing the paper and feather tiara, commented, "I can't wait to call Daddy and tell him we ended the night singing with Kitty Carlisle. I love the way that song ends, Al......ways."

In May, 2005 the beautiful rising pop/rock star EJ (Erin Jividen) made her debut at the Cafe Pierre at Landis' kind invitation, and for a few songs, the Cafe rocked, with an audience that included jazz authority and former New York Post cabaret critic Chip Deffaa, legendary TV and radio talk show host Joe Franklin and Brad Balfour of am New York.

From Manhattan's elegant Hotel Pierre to Legendary Carnegie Hall, glamorous Kathleen Landis continues to expand her circle of enthusiastic audiences. Known for her versatile repertoire, she interprets the great American standards with imagination, reflecting both jazz and classical influences.

Within the intimacy of the Café Pierre, Kathleen weaves a romantic sophistication reminiscent of the days of café society and intimate New York supper clubs. Along with her popular ongoing engagement at the Hotel Pierre, Landis performs a variety of musical programs in and around the New York Area, including the Algonquin Hotel's Oak Room, Steinway Hall, the Tilles Center, and Caramoor Music Room. She has appeared in live performances in Europe, as well as in Canada and The United Arab Emirates, and has been featured on many New York radio and cable television programs.

Landis, acknowledged for her George Gershwin interpretations, celebrated the Gershwin centennial by performing two sold-out concerts with a nine-piece ensemble at Carnegie Hall's Weill Recital Hall. Completing the Gershwin cycle, Landis released her first CD, *Gershwin, Island to Island*, which was received with critical acclaim. This recording showcased her crossover ability, interpreting the many facets of Gershwin's music.

Ms. Landis graciously agreed to provide some anecdotes on The Pierre for this book.

"The Pierre Hotel is many things to many people. One of the most important things that The Pierre represents is romantic memories," the singer told me. "There are three or four separate areas of the hotel that form a whole and yet are dramatically separate. There is rarely an overlap of experience.

"The co-ops are one entity and since they technically own The Pierre, they exert a great deal of influence and control. The Four Seasons became the official management in the early 80's and have remained to the present day. The co-op residents live in approximately 60 percent of the hotel. In my many years as entertainer in the Café, I've come to know many of the owners as personal friends, including Roy Neuberger who turned 100 years on July 21, 2003. (Landis flew in from her vacation to sing and play for the gala occasion.)

"There are many people who have fabulous memories of growing up or living at The Pierre. So often I meet people in the café bar or restaurant who are truly emotional about coming back to the hotel where they find the same doorman, the same bartender who served him their first drink with his father, the same—well, the same hotel with many of the same people. The employees at The Pierre are a throwback to another time in history when a person took a position and remained there until they retired. The first thing I became aware of when I started back in the 80's was the special relationship between the customer and the staff. The staff in the Café knew exactly what a customer wanted, knew their whole family as if they worked for them as part of their household.

"Back in the mid-80's, there was Rita Lachman, who held court and center stage at the bar on a nightly basis. Rita was the ultimate hotel bar character. Her crackling laughter or shriek, which might be heard as one entered the Café, was known to many customers. She was a charming hostess to the whole room, with incredible life stories, both worldly and gay. Unfortunately, she could also be ruthless. In the end, she grew desperate to sell her story, desperate for money, even shelter.

"During the late 80's, the Hotel decided to resume dancing in the Café. This was immediately very popular and brought a new group of Café devotees. One very well dressed mature gentleman began showing up every night. He would always sit directly behind the piano, order and share with me a very good champagne and would listen attentively for hours, oblivious to all the other goings on. I knew he was developing a serious crush even though I told him early on of my unavailability. It was soon after we spent time talking on my breaks that I discovered the very unusual profession that allowed him this nightly indulgence of champagne and Pierre dinners. He is a street salesman, his product, potato peelers!"

Joe, who still sells peelers 3 for $20 everyday on the streets of New York, eventually met a real estate heiress at the bar, fell in love, married and now lives on Park Avenue.

"The Pierre was a center for many of the jet setters during the late 60's through the mid-80's," Kathleen Landis continued her recollections. "Rita Lachman was one of those hostesses who knew everyone in the 'in' crowd who traveled from New York, to Paris, to Rome and Capri. She was technically a neighbor not a resident at The Pierre having moved to 800 Fifth Avenue (across the street from the hotel) after her divorce to Charles Lachman. Lachman was the L in Revlon. One of three original partners in the formation of the company. He was the least known because he was the scientist behind the cosmetics and a relatively non-public kind of millionaire guy. Rita became Mrs. Lachman the 2nd because of her affair with and subsequent pregnancy by Charles Lachman. Legend has it that Rita was trying to convince Charles that he should divorce and marry her for their future child's sake because this would be his only actual heir. Charles' other two children were adopted. She supposedly, while huge with child, marched into the first Mrs. L.'s hair salon and announced she was carrying his child. After his divorce he married Rita and became the proud father of Charlene. Rita, who had worked in ladies dress shops after arriving in this country from Berlin, suddenly became extremely wealthy. During the jet set days of the 60's and 70's, she and Charles owned a yacht and they hung their Monets in a 15 room apartment in Paris that was decorated in Louis IVth style. But all things that go around come around and when Rita found out that Charles was having an affair with her own secretary, she threatened him with divorce and to her dismay and misfortune, he took her up on it. Although she lost the apartment in Paris and the French originals, she received an exorbitant amount in her settlement. This allowed her to continue pretty much her extravagant spending style which included the yacht, a few million and a trust fund which covered her a hundred thousand a year just in case she went overboard on her gambling sprees, which actually did bring her to the state of affairs she was in when I first met her at the Café around '84.

"Although she was living directly across the street on 61st Street, Rita would arrive at the Café as soon as she was up and had her makeup (which included false eyelashes and heavy liner) on. She traveled with several photo albums that included photos of her previous life and the who's who that she hung around with. It was Rita's firm Germanic belief that she was destined to high class living and that her story was so extraordinary, that either she would meet and entrap another very very wealthy, handsome and rich man or that someone she told her story to (usually at the bar after several drinks) would want to buy it for an exorbitant price and make a film or TV series out of it.

"As Rita's money began to run out, she continued to live as if there would be no end to it. She made a lot of investment mistakes. She just couldn't handle it, only spend it. Things were spiraling downward for Rita but she never seemed to doubt that it would turn around again. Her last clump of real money she spent on a face lift and breast augmentation (she was well into her 70's then) then she moved back to Europe where she stayed at one famous hotel after another and always spent her days in their bars carrying her photo albums. She was unable to pay her bills and subsequently was thrown out of all of Europe's best. A few of them kept her trunks and suitcases as collateral for payment. The last story we heard of dear Rita was from a Café Pierre regular who'd been visiting England at one of the best hotel bars and had seen her there holding court. On a later trip he asked the bartender if she was still coming in and the bartender replied with real sadness that even though she owed the hotel a lot of money and even some of the employees, they heard she was in a hospital for the poor and that she had cancer. They went to the hospital to visit her but Rita refused to have them see her."

A true artist, Kathleen Landis is always broadening her horizons. Expanding her live performances to television, she was recently selected as featured actress and jazz pianist in a nationally aired commercial for Advil for which she did the musical arrangements. Kathleen has also been interviewed by Barbara Walters for ABC's "20/20" in a piece that examined the effects of 9/11 on the spirit of the city she calls home.

Landis hosted a musical tribute to Mildred and Peter Hanson, steadfast devotees of cabaret, on the Hansons' 22nd wedding anniversary on December 2, 2004. It showcased cabaret and Broadway performers Julie Wilson, Steve Ross and Daryl Sherman, with famed opera star Deborah Voight chiming in. Ms. Landis accompanied the evening's guest singer, Frank Dain, editor of *Cabaret Scenes* magazine. Performing to a sold-out room, they created an intimate musical soirée reminiscent of the salon evenings of Mabel Mercer. The regular patrons were intoxicatingly surprised by this unannounced panoply of well-known performers, highlighted by Landis playing for New York's premier cabaret diva, Julie Wilson, who sang, "But Beautiful" and Steve Ross who performed "Married" (which, by the way, he'd sung to the Hansons on their wedding night twenty-two years earlier at the Algonquin Hotel's Oak Room). Affectionately known as the Pierre's "Astaire & Rogers," the Hansons then took to the floor, dancing and dipping for a delighted audience, stylishly "Puttin' on the Ritz" or more accurately, "Puttin' on the Pierre."

I visited Roy Neuberger and his fabulous art collection late one afternoon in the fall of 2004 in the company of Ms. Landis, who, if you're very lucky, will play on the grand piano in Mr. Newberger's cavernous living room overlooking Fifth Avenue.

The apartment was once occupied by the late Irene Selznick, daughter of MGM mogul Louis B. Mayer, who married *Gone with the Wind* director David O. Selznick.

Moving from his bedroom to the living room, Mr. Neuberger pointed to a large mobile. "That's a Calder. He was the most charming artist that lived in his time. He lived in Roxbury, Connecticut, and I knew him well. Calder was a wonderful artist. I have another one in the country. A painting."

The talk turned to singers. "Chevalier was really great. Talk about the crooners. He was the best. If we could only invite him to sing one night at the Café Pierre. I always want the impossible!"

Turning to Ms. Landis, he said, "I love you Kathleen," with Ms. Landis responding, "I love you, Roy."

"She's a great lady," he said.

"So, Roy, when will I see you again? When are you coming down to the café?" she asked him. "I missed you last night. I was at Barbara Cook's opening and later she sang without a microphone just in her living room in her apartment on Riverside Drive."

After the death of his wife, Marie, in 1997, Mr. Neuberger published his autobiography, *So Far, So Good*. Kitty Carlyle Hart and Mr. Newberger became closer friends, sometimes traveling together. The ever youthful and ever beautiful Mrs. Hart is five years Mr. Newberger's junior. Mrs. Hart started the chorus of "Happy 100th Birthday" for his centennial birthday party.

"In 1980, I was Director of Banquets at The Pierre Hotel as well as President of the American Symphony Orchestra." Martin Riskin told me. "In the United States symphony orchestras are in constant need of funds, with the A.S.O. not being an exception. At a board meeting of the orchestra I proposed that we hold a benefit at The Pierre with dinner, and entertainment provided by my good friend Victor Borge who generously agreed to perform at a greatly reduced fee.

"When the day of the event arrived, I felt every little detail had been taken care of—but I was mistaken. Victor would only perform with his magnificent Boesendorfer piano, the largest concert grand piano in the world. At about 5:30 p.m. the headwaiter reported to me the terrible news that the piano was still in the freight elevator. We had previously brought in Rolls Royces and other large items, however the size and shape of the piano was causing a huge problem. I contacted the best piano technicians and expert movers who tried to get the instrument out, but it wouldn't budge.

"The format of the party was the cocktail reception at seven, Victor's performance at eight, and dinner at nine. I was in a terrible predicament. With all the pushing and pulling, if the $80,000 piano broke or remained stuck there would be 600 disappointed people who had purchased expensive tickets. On top of this I could lose Victor's friendship, which I treasured, not to mention my job, which I needed.

"To avoid upsetting Victor who was up in his dressing suite, as well as the guests, I instructed the staff not to mention the problem. Finally we found an elevator mechanic who arrived shortly before eight. After viewing the situation he told me the alternatives were either breaking the piano or damaging the elevator. I had to make an immediate decision. If the piano was broken it would be a disaster whereas a damaged elevator hopefully could be fixed later at a reasonable cost. The mechanic was told to do what he could with the elevator. In about 30 minutes he was able to solve the problem with only minor damage to the elevator and the piano was brought into the Grand Ballroom just before we had to open the reception doors for the restless guests. The piano tuner immediately went to work, with many people remarking how charming it was to have this as part of Victor Borge's act!

"A couple of weeks later, after dinner at the Borge's home in Greenwich, Connecticut, Victor and I took a walk around their estate. He mentioned how receptive the audience was at The Pierre and his pleasure to help the American Symphony Orchestra. Little did he know what we went through that night."

CHAPTER 10

THE CARLYLE,
"PRINCESS DIANA'S FAVORITE"

Woody Allen calls The Carlyle "one of the city's great icons." Actors from James O'Neill (Eugene O'Neill's father, who toured the county in *The Count of Monte Christo*) to Robert De Niro and Will Rogers have liked to stay in hotels because of their comfort and service. Actress Elaine Stritch lives at the Carlyle and she told *Newsday* that the hotel is "a relaxed elegance without being too upper-crusty. They're not trying too hard. That's the greatest sign of talent in any profession."

New York City, like London, Paris, Rome, Moscow and other centers of international renown, is a town of walkers and taxicabs and other forms of public transportation. No one knows this better than the celebrities of politics, business and culture who must visit these destinations in order to keep civilization as we know it alive. Once these people arrive, they, however celebrated, must find a place to rest: to live, to converse, to eat, and to meet each other in social events. For many decades the place they have chosen in New York City has been The Carlyle, the 35-story hotel located on Madison Avenue within sight of Central Park and within easy distance of much that New York City has to offer.

There is no quieter or more quietly discreet place to be found in this frequently turbulent city. It has been the hotel of choice for several American Presidents since it was built by the entrepreneurial developer Moses Ginsberg in the 1920's. Completed in 1929 by the architects Bien & Prince at 35 East 76th Street (extending to 77th Street on Madison Avenue between Madison and Park Avenues) it has been host to many of America's international allies and even its adversaries. In fact, the Carlyle Hotel once nearly accomplished the feat which the CIA vainly strove to achieve (apparently) for years—it nearly assassinated Mr. Castro, and in the company of Khrushchev to boot. The two Communist titans once shared an elevator at the hotel which almost crashed because of the overloaded cargo of their combined burly protectors and aides.

While The Carlyle is perhaps not so well known in a popular sense as, for example, The Waldorf-Astoria or The Plaza, it's widely celebrated among world leaders, and some entertainment stars, who appreciate its extreme sense of discretion as much as its attention to the comforts of important travelers. Moreover, it's revered by New Yorkers themselves, among them the famous Brooke Astor, doyenne of this city's society and a determined philanthropist.

Brooke Astor attended her first "New York City party" there shortly after The Carlyle was built, and in 1997 Brendan Gill wrote of a memorable birthday celebration in her honor:

> "The invitation to the party stipulated eight o'clock and black tie, and I approach the Café Carlyle at precisely eight, wearing a purple bow tie that serves as my version of black. It began snowing earlier in the day, and now the wind is rising. On Madison Avenue, umbrellas are blowing inside out, and the snow, as it strikes the sidewalk, turns into slush. I had expected the party to start late because of the storm, but no. Although many of Brooke's friends are elderly, they have long since demonstrated their physical toughness; they are survivors, who believe (as Zelda Fitzgerald once wrote) that weather is for children. In they come, shaking the snow off their hats and coats, stamping their boots on the marble floor of the vestibule. Cocktails are being served in the oval interior space of the hotel, which is known as the Gallery. Within a few minutes the space is as jam-packed as a subway car at rush hour, and evidently that is the way everyone wishes it to be. There is much laughter amid exclamations of delight at recognizing old friends, and this is odd, because most of the guests encounter one another at parties at least once or twice a week and have been doing so for decades. Nevertheless, their delight appears to be authentic, and all the more intense because of the person whose birthday they are celebrating.

"Where's Brooke?" The recurrent question is answered with a gesture, indicating the point at which she was last seen. As usual, Brooke is making an effort to be everywhere at once, and because she is small, she is nearly invisible as she threads her way through the crowd. She is wearing a long evening dress of dark green velvet—"A fine dress to dance in; I can kick up my heels"—and around her throat is a necklace of large diamonds in a platinum setting.

…Bobby Short seats himself at the piano, saying, "Whenever Brooke comes here to the Café, I play a certain favorite song of hers." He launches bouncily into Cole Porter's "Just One of Those Things." I think of Cole and Linda Porter and Brooke and Buddy Marshall dining in Paris, in the Porters' suave house on the Rue Monsieur, a long time ago…

…The hour is late. Beyond the windows, snow is falling and is expected to continue falling throughout the night. Here in the Café, everything is safe against the storm. And Brooke is dancing.

The Carlyle mirrors an American Century of politics, power, and glamour. It's also an intimate composite portrait of the multitude of celebrated and internationally powerful figures who have considered The Carlyle their home in New York, from Diana, Princess of Wales, to John F. Kennedy and Harry Truman, to Yankees owner George Steinbrenner, and many others who prefer the legendary privacy of this hostelry on East 76th Street. How many stories can those walls reveal?

Diana, Princess of Wales, ostracized from the British Royal Family, found a home away from the home she never had at The Carlyle, where she exhibited a queenly grace. The Kings and Queens of Denmark, Greece, Italy, Spain and Sweden have also visited. While royalty enjoyed the tower views, families visiting New York for debutante and bridal parties could indeed partake of the popular appeal of residential hotels in the 1920's which promised "freedom from drudgery, the servant problem, plus the many responsibilities that go with maintaining large private houses," as one newspaper account said at the time.

"This was her favorite place to stay in America," Michael O'Connell, a longtime bellboy at The Carlyle, told me of his experience with Princess

Di. "In fact, Mr. (James) Sherwin, our resident manager, he was English. He used to tell me, 'Michael, be ready in 10 minutes. The Princess is coming.' I used to go up here to the left and bring her through the florist. Around to the front.

"I'd take her overnight bag and lead the way and there was always a guy from Scotland Yard with her. She'd come in the back entrance, 77th Street. And she'd come through that door right by the florist shop, through the lobby and then up. (Not through the front lobby.) Each time she came in we took her upstairs. She was standing like that and I said, 'Princess, it's so good to have you back again.' She said, 'I love it here. Thank you very much.' She came with that Scotland Yard man and she also had a lady in waiting."

Princess Diana loved staying at The Carlyle so much that she considered buying an apartment there before her tragic death. She once braved an onslaught of photographers to receive a bouquet of flowers from a little boy who'd waited patiently for hours to catch a glimpse of the Princess and perhaps even present her his bouquet. Diana, Princess of Wales, ostracized by her British Royal Family at home, always exhibited a quiet gravity and genuine concern for others at The Carlyle.

I asked Michael O'Connell if Prince Charles ever accompanied her.

"The Prince stayed here after it was all over with. He was here a couple of years ago (with Camilla Parker-Bowles). But if the H.R.H., the Prince of Wales, stayed at The Carlyle during an official visit, the Princess made it her home. She lived here."

Peter Sharp hand-picked Frank Bowling to run the hotel and many say it has never been run as graciously or efficiently since. "I was there ten years altogether but in two five-year increments," Mr. Bowling told me. "The first time was 1979 to 1984."

Mr. Bowling worked at The Connaught in London before he was at The Carlyle and then ran the Bel-Air in Los Angeles. He, more than most managers, knows how interrelated many hotels are—like extended members of a nevertheless close-knit family. "All these hotels understand each other...They are more like clubs than hotels because they have the same clientele. Everybody just comes from the Bel-Air on their way to The Carlyle. I just want to make a point about what you were saying about the service. The Carlyle was privately owned for many years. Even before it was owned by Peter Sharp and his family it was very much a personal, hands-on hotel..."

"The Sharps owned an antique store and they would change the décor in the lobby twice a year…Peter Sharp was a client of mine at The Connaught, which is how I got the job at The Carlyle. And he stayed at the Bel-Air in Los Angeles. He was there throughout my whole tenure. My whole time there he was the owner.

"As a matter of fact he considered that his home. So if guests were staying at the hotel…(Carlyle) it was like they were staying at his home. Going back to the idea of the lack of a (Grand) function room, it wasn't built as a grand hotel; it was built as a residential hotel. People giving up their townhouses and moving out to the country and they just needed a pied-a-terre, and the dining room strictly for the use of the people who lived there…It's known in all the right circles. It's one of those hotels that when people ask, 'Where are you staying?' and you say, 'The Carlyle,' and they say, 'Oh!' It's that kind of place…I had to train myself not to pick up pieces of paper on the carpet when I was walking guests around. Then I would go back and pick it up later—MBWA. MBWA. It's called management by walking around. That was Peter's philosophy. You never knew when he was coming in. He might have gone to the country on Saturday and come back early on Sunday afternoon, and say, 'Let's have a look around, Frank!'

"We'd walk around the hotel and view rooms at random and check them. He had kind of mental white gloves and he'd walk into a room and 'sweep it.' He'd check out all these places—behind the toilet. Under the bed. Whatever. If he found something he wasn't sharp-tongued to anyone about it. He offered the help a gentle reminder…

"Dan Camp was there a long time—close to 15 years. He's doing other things now." Mr. Bowling seems somewhat shocked by this turn of events. "Going to another hotel would be 'second rate'" is how he feels himself.

"Peter Sharp was absolutely brilliant," Ronald Hestor told me. "They called it 'Peter's Place.' And you'd find him at 7 o'clock in the morning down in room service looking to see what's going on. He said to one of our former resident managers that he believed in 'management by walking around!' He wasn't on the property all the time. Obviously he was also running his real estate empire. But he lived around the corner so he knew what was going on. He wanted to see if the breakfast was getting up promptly, all that sort of thing."

Although she lists her main business as "investments," Caroline Rose Hunt, the daughter of Texas oil baron H.L. Hunt, has been a major force in the luxury hotel business. The Honorary Chairman of Rosewood Hotels & Resorts, she has set new standards in hotel luxury and service, first with the Mansion on Turtle Creek and later with the Lanesborough in London and The Carlyle in New York. Her genial laugh and graciousness masks an indomitable dedication to excellence. Her name is now synonymous with top flight hotels like Claridge's in London or The Plaza or Waldorf Towers, not to mention The Carlyle, which Rosewood manages. She launched her flagship property, The Mansion of Turtle Creek in 1980, the first in what became a pure platinum chain or "group" of hotels. Her story is also a microcosm of second generation American enterprise at its best. The daughter of tough Texas oil czar H.L. Hunt never settles for second best; yet she remains the same sweet, concerned and unaffected individual she was at the Hockaday School in Dallas and the University of Texas after that.

Caroline Hunt's innate understanding of hospitality also grew out of her extraordinarily rich lifestyle. When childhood friend Dorothy Haggard visited "Mount Vernon," the Hunt's family mansion on White Rock Lake outside of Dallas, she got to sleep in Ms. Hunt's bed on cotton sheets that were the finest ever made.

"It's a very complicated thing and the newspapers have never gotten it right—even here in Dallas," Ms. Hunt told me about her involvement in the hotel biz in an interview in her Dallas office. "There is a company called Maritz, Wolff & Company (headed by Phillip or "Flip" Maritz) and they have a hotel arm and they have bought many of the Fairmont Hotels. They owned half of the Fairmonts and Prince Alwaleed was for some 16 years a partner in the Fairmonts. Anyway, we knew about them and they knew about us. So we negotiated. What we did is we put one half of our management company and one half of The Mansion on Turtle Creek in a new venture they had formed. One reason is we wanted to expand Rosewood but didn't want to put up too much money into it."

The office is in the same hotel and office complex she lives in. Ms. Hunt went on to tell me that she "stayed at The Carlyle before we took over the management contract."

Will it be a problem if The Carlyle becomes a better hotel than The Mansion?

"You have to take what comes. And that would be a nice thing to take! With those Diamond Awards what they choose is a very big hotel, a medium hotel and a small hotel. We have had a five-diamond restaurant as well as a five-diamond hotel. That's something we try to emphasize in all of our properties. Frankly, when The Mansion started it did not have very good food.

"It was also the first of what we called residential hotels. We later built these apartments (a separate apartment tower). Then we decided to have the 21 Club there because they were very successful. They enabled us to have lots of people and if there is one thing I've learned, if you have the best hotel or restaurant in the world, unless you get the word out you'll do no business."

Ms. Hunt told me that, these days, "I have nothing to do with the operation of The Carlyle, just policy and public relations. Aside from that I have five children. I suppose I really work for Rosewood's public relations department!"

Dan Camp, a dapper, detail-oriented hotel man, took over management of The Carlyle after Peter Sharp died. One of his innovations (before the Internet, of course) was to install direct telephone lines in some rooms to Sotheby's across the street, directly across Madison Avenue.

"We're trying to be very, very careful not to take anything away from the hotel because it is an institution," Ms. Hunt told me shortly after Rosewood took over The Carlyle management.

Most hotel observers say The Carlyle couldn't be in better hands.

"I've known Caroline since I was 15," recalls Vicky Howland, who was once married to one of Caroline's sons. And she has such a gift at hospitality even before she got involved in the hotel business. I can remember going to her house for dinner. And the way she entertained. She loved having family together."

Dorothy Haggard, a Dallasite and friend, has known Caroline since they were girls in school together. "Caroline hasn't changed since I first knew her. She's remained the same sweet lovely person," Haggard told me.

Vicky Howland continued, in a vein that's important to the telling of The Carlyle story and its strong Texas connection:

"It's not just a business to her. It's the love she has for making people feel comfortable and making people feel at home. It's a wonderful gift that she has been able to expand for all of us to enjoy."

"And I didn't pay her to say that either," Caroline chimed in with her quick and self-effacing sense of humor.

"Caroline Hunt has a great reputation in the hotel business," chimes in Martin Riskin, a hotelier who worked at The Plaza, The Pierre and St. Regis in top executive positions.

The Carlyle is today a microcosm of American creativity and inge-
nuity. Dwarfed by both The Plaza and The Waldorf in sheer size and
numbers of rooms, The Carlyle is nevertheless the epicenter of history,
society and celebrity. It's where the politically powerful live, eat and chat
up Hollywood and Wall Street kings, queens and princesses. Society doyen
Brooke Astor may have given her regards to The Plaza for its 75th anniversary in 1982 but when it came time to celebrate her 95th birthday it was at
The Carlyle. Today, it's also where scenes of the coming and going of the
political and industrial elite are now part of our national psyche: It's Home-
land Security Director Tom Ridge meeting behind closed doors, as a knight
of the moneyed Manhattan elite and the general American populace.

Of course, for a long time The Carlyle has been best known for the
quality of its entertainment in the Café Carlyle. Most notably, pianist and
singer Bobby Short, was the biggest cabaret star in New York since
Hildegarde. In recent years, Woody Allen has played jazz there every
Monday night to similarly packed houses.

I had once done a front page story in The New York *Post* about the
possibility that Woody and Mia Farrow would patch up some of their
differences. After the story broke, I was asked to try to interview Woody
himself about it and he told me he would "in a moment." Then he asked
me who I was with and I suddenly felt chicken that I was with The New
York *Post* and I said, "People.com" which I was also working for at the
time. For a little fellow, he's a very imposing figure, especially when you
remember that despite some of his well-publicized problems he's still one
of our great cinematic geniuses.

Perhaps one of the biggest ironies about The Carlyle is that Ludwig
Bemelmans, a maverick, an outsider, an artist and writer who became
independently wealthy after his "Madelaine" books were published, and
someone who said he sometimes preferred third class to first class during
transatlantic crossings, is so linked with the Carlyle, a bastion of tradition
and upper-class conformity. While he cunningly worked out a deal to
paint murals of Central Park in the hotel's bar in exchange for staying in
its penthouse suite for over a year, one wonders if the incorrigible bohe-
mian would have been permitted to stay in it under any other circumstances, even if he'd had the money.

"The most 'unique' faces at the Splendide belonged to Monsieur
and Madame Lawrance Potter Dreyspool," Ludwig Bemelmans wrote in
his *Hotel Splendide*. "Madame Dreyspool was very rich; her husband was

not. He traveled with her as a sort of companion-butler, pulling her chair, helping her to get up, carrying books, flasks, dog leashes, small purchases, and opera glasses. He was also like the attendant at a sideshow, for Madame was a monstrosity and everyone stared at her. They both were very fat but she was enormous." Clearly, neither would have fit in very well at the Carlyle!

Another irony involving the Carlyle and its artistic penthouse-dweller Bemelmans is that the residential feeling is in stark contrast to the lands of glimmering palaces he often wrote about. In reviewing *Hotel Bemelmans*, which Ebury Press published in 2003, James Pinero, writing in the New York *Sun*, concluded that "The grand hotel represents the bygone era of high luxury. The species of luxury that existed in the finest hotels of the world between the wars rooted itself in the fertile imagination of Ludwig Bemelmans." He talks in the book of Mrs. George Washington Kelly's birthday party at one of these hotels in which "Madame had decided to build at the end of the ballroom a replica of her Miami retreat, 'O Sole Mio,' in its original dimensions…surrounded by 40 three-foot palm trees and fronted by wide terraces."

Compared to some of New York's other hotel palaces, the physical building of The Carlyle was more or less the work of one man, Moses Ginsberg, a Russian immigrant who made his early fortune in Brooklyn real estate. He built the hotel in only 13 months, patterning it extensively on prominent Fifth and Park Avenue cooperative apartment buildings, including 740 Park Avenue, which is one of Manhattan's very best residential buildings. Ginsberg's daughter, Diana Ginsberg Jaffe, proposed calling it The Carlyle after English writer Thomas Carlyle and Moses' son, Calmon, assisted with the hotel's construction. But only two years after The Carlyle opened in 1930, Ginsberg, who had adopted the common hotel policy of luring celebrities to stay there rent free (among them composer Richard Rodgers), lost his brick-and-steel 'love child' to the banks, which had foreclosed on the property. But by then the Sylvan Bien design scheme and the Dorothy Draper interior had been embraced by Manhattan's social, political and entertainment elite.

Composer Mary Rodgers, the daughter of the late Richard Rodgers, doesn't recall that her dad ever got his suite at The Carlyle rent free. "He lived in hotels," she told me "before he was married and after he was married when I was a baby. Then he went to California. Then they lived back in the apartment side of The Carlyle. They had already rented that apartment and left to go to California and come back. Then he went to Connecticut. Then they bought an apartment at 730 Park Avenue and then they went to The Pierre." She also said that the "apartment side of The Carlyle was not a hotel (even though it had hotel services.) It was a regular apartment building on 77th Street. He lived at the Lombardy as a bachelor. Edna Ferber lived there."

Enter Robert Dowling. Like Ginsberg, he ran the Carlyle less as a business and more as a rich man's toy.

Dorothy Draper, who'd already cut a wide swath through New York decorating in the 1920's, was the hotel's first interior decorator. "Today, her strong Art Deco influence has been painstakingly maintained," a recent hotel press release proclaimed, "The late Mark Hampton has updated many of the guest rooms with a contemporary interpretation of the understated elegance achieved by Dorothy Draper 70 years ago."

Perhaps that explains why the Carlyle's public spaces are much smaller than those of The Plaza, The Waldorf or even The Pierre. Suitable for more serene affairs, the gilt and chandeliers give way more to those who relish quiet elegance and a sort of social isolation.

In a way, this made writing about The Carlyle more difficult than I first assumed when the research and writing of this book began. Having written about The Plaza and the Waldorf-Astoria, which had public rooms that were on a par with some of the great houses and castles of Europe, I saw a difference. The big rooms at the bigger hotels attracted glittering balls and weddings like Truman Capote's famous "Black and White Ball." The Carlyle, however, had no such grand spaces although some of its parties, like Brooke Astor's 95th birthday, could hold their own with those at The Pierre, Waldorf-Astoria and The Plaza.

Whatever its size, the hotel has set universally praised standards, and under Rosewood managements is poised to become one of the world's most respected hotels. Its celebrated guests, from Winston Churchill to Princess Diana, have always been more than willing to attest to its excellence. And who would know better than they?

"Happy Birthday, Mr. President"

After President Kennedy's historic birthday party at Madison Square Garden, during which Marilyn Monroe sang "Happy Birthday, Mr. President" in a voice at once childlike and sexy, Monroe slipped into The Carlyle for what hotel sources say was Kennedy and Monroe's last night together before Monroe's death in 1962.

"So many people have stayed here over the years and you think of them as hotel guests more than as celebrities," says longtime executive assistant manager Ronald Hestor. "It's a little frightening, when you do think of the people you deal with on a day-to-day basis. The Jack Lemmons used to be here. And at one time we had both Maestro Sir George Solti, Hungarian born, and the Austrian Maestro Herbert von Karajan, at the same time. People would ask for the maestro and they'd get the wrong one.

"I was standing behind the desk one night. This probably is 1966. And Audrey Hepburn was staying in the hotel, looking absolutely fabulous. Jackie had lived here. She was here for a year after the assassination while the apartment on Fifth was being done. And, of course, she had stayed here when Jack was President. And she would come to lunch and she would even come and use the pay phone. So Audrey was sitting in the corner. And Jackie came either out of the dining room or out of the pay phone. Saw her sitting in the lobby and she went over and talked to her."

CHAPTER 11
POLITICIANS AND THE CARLYLE, WALDORF AND ALL

John F. Kennedy stayed in a duplex, 38A, while both Nancy Reagan and Jacqueline Kennedy, as widows, preferred suite 1812, which had three bedrooms.

Former President Harry Truman would leisurely write to his former aide Dean Acheson of his joy of his daughter's impending marriage to a man he described as "a very nice fellow."

"The young lady told us about it just a week or two before the announcement and swore us to secrecy," he wrote in one letter to Acheson. "In fact, she made me hang up while she told her mother…(since then) we've had at least two thousand letters and telegrams and she's had twice as many—serves her right."

In short, the Carlyle Hotel has long been the home away from home for U.S. Presidents and international political leaders from President Kennedy, Nancy and President Reagan to Prime Minister Nehru of India. And while it has set undeniable standards itself as a hotel, it also has helped shape American and world history.

When I did my book on The Waldorf I was told by then manager Eugene Scanlan that Monroe visited Kennedy at The Waldorf as well. He said she came up to his suite via the service elevator. "How did you know she did?" I asked Scanlan. "I brought her up myself!" he told me.

A favorite guest among the Carlyle staff was former President Reagan. "I have a photograph of myself taken with Mr. and Mrs. Ronald Reagan. It doesn't get any better than that!" However, this manager added that, "Mr. Reagan was not one to come and chat at the front desk."

Presidents are the preferred guests at The Carlyle. Royalty ranks somewhere lower, especially those who fail to pay their bills. There was one King Peter of Yugoslavia, who was bankrolled by a group of businessmen in Chicago who were operating in the vain hope that he would someday assume the throne. His bill was never fully paid.

Mrs. Ferdinand Marcos of the Philippines did pay her bills—in a rather odd way. With suitcases of $10 and $20 bills. No one asked where they came from.

On May 19, 1962, the world learned of Marilyn Monroe's devotion to Jack Kennedy. Wearing a $12,000 Jean Louis silk beaded dress Monroe sang "Happy Birthday, Mr. Pres-i-dent" in her own inimitable way. After her song, President Kennedy told the audience, "I can now retire from politics after having 'Happy Birthday' sung to me in such a sweet and wholesome way." But far from the cheering crowds, their relationship later that night was anything but sweet and wholesome. They both attended a gala at the home of Arthur Krim, the Democratic Party leader. But "shortly after 1:00 A.M., Secret Service agents escorted the President, the movie star and a handful of others through the crowded apartment and into a private elevator, which descended to the basement of Krim's apartment house," Nellie Bly wrote in *The Kennedy Men: Three Generations of Sex, Scandal and Secrets*. "From there they moved through a series of tunnels that connected the Carlyle Hotel with nearby apartment houses."

Monroe and Kennedy then took a private elevator into The Carlyle penthouse. Gossip columnist Earl Wilson wrote that, "It was the last prolonged encounter between them." JFK's hasty encounters took a cue from his father's affairs. Gloria Swanson, in her memoirs, said about her first time alone with Joe Kennedy, Sr., at the Royal Poinciana Hotel in Florida, that "He moved so quickly that his mouth was on mine before either of us could speak. With one hand he held the back of my head, with the other he stroked my body and pulled at my kimono. He kept insisting in a drawn-out moan, 'No longer, no longer. Now!'"

JFK, too, engaged in ultra quick encounters with many women at The Carlyle, sources told me. One after another, like people waiting at the checkout counter, women would enter his room there. To top it all off, these sources said, there were other women who were tipped off on exactly which windows to look at with their binoculars on the Southeast corner of the building.

"I knew two girls that were run through the process," one source told me. "And I can tell you everything was easily arranged. They would simply bring a young lady up from the floor below." And when Kennedy had finished with one woman, another was ushered into his room.

These were very well-born women. I'll tell you the procedure and how it was a set-up. The U.S. Secret Service was working 24 hours a day. The man who was the head was David Powers and he was very close to The President and went to work for him in the days he was trying to become a Congressman. David Powers was the one in charge of that kind of thing."

Whatever went on behind closed doors—and apparently in full view of some high society—Kennedy always remained popular with the staff of The Carlyle. Two weeks before he was assassinated in Dallas he told the staff, which had assembled in the lobby, "I'll see you in two weeks!"

One reliable source said the back stairway of the hotel was an unusually busy place when Kennedy was at the hotel.

If sex was the first order of pleasure for Kennedy, dignity and laughter were the hallmarks of another Brahmin of society. For example, it was only natural that Brooke Astor celebrate her 95th birthday at The Carlyle in an atmosphere that was similar to dinner parties in her red-brick Georgian apartment house on Park Avenue in the 70's. It was a dark and stormy night outside. Inside, in the warm candlelight, friends gathered to salute the woman who had done so much to save Manhattan landmarks (with money from her late husband, Vincent Astor) like the Villard Houses at Madison Avenue at 51st Street.

The first hotel Truman and his wife, Bess, stayed in New York after his Presidency was The Waldorf-Astoria when they took a leisurely car trip from Independence, Missouri to Washington, DC and up to New York. They saw Leonard Bernstein's *Wonderful Town* on Broadway and were given a standing ovation as they took their seats in the Winter Garden Theatre. "Cab drivers in New York did not just call to him, they pulled to the curb and jumped out to shake his hand," recounted David McCullough, in *Truman*, his biography of the American President. Truman himself wrote a lot of his own memoirs while living at the Carlyle Hotel in apartment 10A, where he drove the Secret Service crazy by taking walks up Madison Avenue and attracting big crowds, including the press, by himself.

President Kennedy was lured to the hotel initially not by a blonde, brunette or redhead, but by owner Robert Dowling, a prominent Democratic Party fundraiser, who preferred its more private, off-the-beaten-track elegance to the fishbowl atmosphere of the Waldorf-Astoria and its exclusive Waldorf Towers apartments on the 50th Street side of that hotel.

C. Delany Howland, a Dallas investment banker, now married to Caroline Hunt's former daughter-in-law, recalls living at The Carlyle when he was a child.

"When my parents got divorced I moved in with my grandparents at 18 East 87th Street. They had a wonderful townhouse near Fifth Avenue. When grandpa died—he died in 1956—grandma kept a house in the country and moved to The Carlyle Hotel. Grandpa got his hair cut there and I did, too…Anyway, we moved in and she got a suite on the 10th floor and it was on the Southwest corner. Two bedrooms. A dining room and a living room. I moved in with her and spent about two years there. I was going to boarding school at the time and I'd come down on vacation. And what happened was that basically I decided I was a little too close to my grandmother. I was a teenager at the time and so she arranged for me to have a room of my own on the 10th floor. And I'd come in at odd times. And there's a room on the 10th floor called 10A. And 10A was reserved for Harry Truman so they always kept it open."

Mr. Howland went on to say that when his grandmother moved into The Carlyle she took some huge portraits of family ancestors with her. The only problem was they were too big to fit upright on the walls of their suite so some had to be tipped slightly at an angle to fit on the walls.

Milton Petrie, of the Petrie stores, owned 34A, paying at one time $120,000 a year in maintenance. Broadway actress, dancer and choreographer Ann Reinking occupied suite 3407 with her husband, Herbert Allen. Ms. Reinking, who had installed a bay window in her eat-in kitchen, would walk "Broadway," a black mutt, or ask Michael O'Conner, the bellman, to walk him with Mr. Allen paying Mr. O'Conner by check weekly.

"I used to run Kennedy up and down in the elevator when he was here," bellman Michael O'Conner told me. "I have a picture with Jackie Kennedy when I was on the elevators. They took our picture and they sent me a copy of it…Audrey Hepburn used to stay here all the time. Ginger Rogers used to stay here. When I first started Harry Truman used to stay here. Very pleasant. Suite 10A. His wife was very nice, Bess. And his daughter…In fact, she used to live here at the time. She had a place on Park Avenue and she used to come to lunch all the time."

"One time Mr. Reagan was alone without Nancy and he sat down and wrote a note in his own hand just how much he loved staying here and so forth," Mr. Hestor told me. "That's the kind of man he was."

Michael O'Connell tells of the times when the lobby would be full of people when Kennedy was here. "George Markum, who was general manager at the time, told me the story about the first time Kennedy was here. Of course, the place was just buzzing. He was about to check out. Markum was front office manager then. The phone rings and he picks it up and says, 'Reception desk, Mr. Markum speaking.' 'Hello, Mr. Markum, this is President Kennedy. I just wanted to tell you how much we enjoyed our visit.' And Mr. Markum practically fell on the floor.

"My first day," Michael O'Connell continued, "I told them what I intended to do, that I'd like the evening shift to finish school, go to high school in the Bronx. I remember the service manager taking me and saying, 'You're to be helping with the mail.' And the packages came in, they'd tell you where to take them. I said, 'O.K.' So I took my time. I delivered packages of mail. That was my first job in the back. Then they brought me up in the elevator and the assistant manager said to me, 'You're now a bellman. The other bellman didn't show up today. You'd better get your gloves on. You're going on the floor.' I can remember that day well. I said, 'Me on the floor? I don't know anything about it.' 'Yes, you do. You greet people when they come in and things like that.' The first diplomat I met was Mendes France. And, of course, everything had to be changed for him (the dignitary). The steps coming down the front stares had gray carpet. The red carpet was put down. In the elevator, there were black and white tiles. Red carpet was put down…And they're still there…I was born in Ireland and came over here when I was 17. I lived with my aunt and uncle and cousins. I stayed with them. It was like home to me…near Parkchester…I started here in 1949 when I came from Ireland."

CHAPTER 12

THE WALDORF-ASTORIA

The new Waldorf at 50th and Park Avenue opened the same day as The Pierre, October 1, 1931. It was the last word in Art Deco splendor, a $42 million dollar palace that couldn't be replicated for less than several billion dollars today.

In the old days, when dozens of transatlantic passenger ships would pull into New York harbor, you could actually see the ships docked at the piers from the upper floors of the hotel. Now there are so many tall buildings in the way you're lucky, if you have a suite on the north side of the hotel, to be able to see Central Park ten blocks to the north.

In any case, as an inducement to get celebrity guests, and publicity from them, the Waldorf gave many big guests a big break on their bills. Elsa Maxwell, the queen of New York party givers, was one of these. And her "April in Paris Ball" became the stuff of legends. But it was her "barnyard parties" that were considered more fun. Parts of the Grand Ballroom were converted into holding pens for various animals, including cows, which Elsa hand-milked. But the highlight of the evening was when Elsa rode in on an elephant. The press was poised for the shot—and in the rather chubby Elsa came mounted atop a pachyderm. That is, until the year the bubble burst when one photographer shouted at the top of his lungs, "Which one is Elsa?!"

Lucius Boomer, who had been the manager of the old Waldorf at 34th Street and Fifth Avenue, was basically the brains behind building the new Waldorf. He'd regularly "walk the hotel," as it was called, inspecting everything from the Penthouse to the subbasement, where there was a train platform into which President Franklin D. Roosevelt's private rail car would glide just before the President himself would be whisked up to, appropriately enough, the Presidential suite.

A tireless worker, Boomer instructed his staff never to call him after 2:00 a.m. in his cavernous suite, including a 40-foot-long living room, unless there was a fire in the hotel. So one night when he was roused at 2:30 a.m. he asked, "Where's the fire?!" It wasn't a fire, his timid assistant retorted. "Not a fire!" Boomer bellowed back. "I thought I told you not to disturb me?" "It's Mr. Cugat (flamboyant bandleader Xavier Cugat). He's bowling outside the elevators on his floor with two women and they're all naked!" "I'll be right there," Boomer said.

My father and mother lived at The Waldorf when I was born. My father was visited by the hotel's lawyer, a John Sherry, who'd been doing some investigating into my father's room service bills to see how he could help him reduce them.

"One thing that would cut your monthly bills by two-thirds would be to order liquor by the bottle instead of by the drink," Mr. Sherry suggested.

"My God, what a brilliant idea!" my father exclaimed. "If you're that good a lawyer I want you to be mine!"

Winston Churchill, obviously, didn't have to worry about his bills at The Waldorf. Even a dead body didn't faze him. Apparently, one of his watchguards died during the night right outside the great man's door. The hotel sent someone to remove the body but not before Churchill was up and out of his suite. As he stepped over the body he asked police to assure the man's relatives he had nothing to do with his death.

Of course, at most of the hotels you've read about in these pages no request is too much for the staff. When a lady arrived at The Waldorf with her pet alligator, the bellmen may have recoiled but the hotel's carpenters wasted no time fashioning a ramp from her bathroom floor to the top of the tub to make it possible for the ungainly green pet to take a bath on his own. This request was similar to one Vito Belfuri, a former carpenter at The Plaza, received to screw in a leg. Going up to the room he assumed it was the leg of a chair. When he arrived, it turned out to be a gentleman's wooden artificial leg.

Until the New York Hilton and Sheraton Hotels were built The Waldorf boasted the most hotel rooms. It still has some of the most lavish suites. Cole Porter lived in a huge 10-room suite in the Waldorf Towers. Frank Sinatra paid some $1 million a year for the same suite in the 1960's.

The movie *Weekend at the Waldorf*, a remake of sorts of *Grand Hotel*, and starring Ginger Rogers, helped make the Waldorf an international icon.

Sinatra died in 1998, though his long association with the hotel as the more or less permanent occupant of 33A, the famed "Cole Porter Suite," described in one of his signature songs, "New York, New York," had ceased several years before that.

Mr. Porter's presence in the hotel, a sort of benign ghost, seems as much a fixture today as the ornate "silver corridor" or artist Simmon's 1893 painting of *"The Season"* in that same illustrious walkway.

Marilyn Monroe, who once rode the service elevator to see President Kennedy in his suite, also lived at the fabled hotel for a time. Nancy Miracle, Marilyn Monroe's daughter, though never acknowledged publicly, says in her play *Here I am Mother*, that she'd visit her mother at the Waldorf. "My mother had a suite there. We'd go there after class. I knew the back door, the stairwells, the kitchens, and I remember a big sign in the kitchen, something about time, 'the impossible takes time...'"

Maurice Chevalier made his farewell New York appearance in the Empire Room and song-and-dance man George M. Cohan did a little soft-shoe and sang a verse from his *Yankee Doodle Dandy* in his final public performance from the stage of the Grand Ballroom. And Cole Porter in 33A "was already dressed and seated at the dining room table," as Jones Harris, who was invited to dinner at Porter's apartment several times, recalled. Asked who most she would like to have at a dinner party, longtime Towers resident Elsa Maxwell said, "Noel Coward on my left and Cole Porter on my right."

That the new Waldorf became a magnet for celebrities in the first place is due in part to the original Waldorf-Astoria's pre-eminence as a favorite of George M. Cohan, Maude Adams (the first Peter Pan) and Sinclair Lewis.

Novelist Sinclair Lewis loved to dine with his publishing buddies in the ornate old grill room of the old Waldorf-Astoria Hotel. In fact, when he lived at 309 Fifth Avenue, a little more than a block from the hotel, in 1915, it was still at the height of its reputation. Little did Sinclair Lewis know that his own country house, "Twin Farms," in Barnard, Vermont, was destined to become one of the plushest hotels in the world, with 16 rooms starting at $1,100 a night, meals inclusive.

Although some of its permanent clientele had been siphoned off by The Plaza, the Waldorf-Astoria at this time, circa 1916, was still managed by George Boldt, who didn't die until the following year, and it was still four years away from Prohibition. The latter took a huge bite out of the city's hotel profits in general and led to the closing of the Knickerbocker as well as serious financial problems for the Waldorf-Astoria.

In my book about the Plaza, I revealed a world of glamour and celebrity that may be unsurpassed in America. Over two dozen major motion pictures have been shot at the Plaza, including *Home Alone II, The Way We Were*, and *North by Northwest*. And yet, few places in New York have seen as much history at the Waldorf-Astoria. To be sure, films like *Scent of a Woman*, with Al Pacino, *Maid in Manhattan*, with Jennifer Lopez and Ralph Fiennes, and *Weekend at the Waldorf*, with Ginger Rogers and Walter Pidgeon, have been filmed at the Waldorf. But, like the White House, there was and is something almost presidential in stature about the Waldorf-Astoria. After all, every President since Franklin D. Roosevelt has stayed in the Art Deco palace. There has even been something patriotic about its movies. When he was stationed in the South Pacific during World War II, Anthony Rey, who'd worked at the Waldorf-Astoria prior to the war, was summoned to a private screening of *Weekend at the Waldorf* with a military escort.

The Waldorf-Astoria was so famous at one point that humorist James Thurber's mother, living in Columbus, Ohio, asked her son "If it was possible for you to take me to lunch at the Waldorf?" Thurber later said that "From the tentative way she put it, I could see why she had never asked me before. She was afraid I couldn't swing it!"

There's also the story of the wealthy manufacturer who met an exotic looking woman in the lobby of the Waldorf. He smiled. She smiled back but spoke no English. So they started to communicate by sketching on a pad. He drew a taxi and they went to the Stork Club nightclub. He drew a couple dancing and they danced. It was her turn and she drew a Louis IV bed. And, he thought to himself, "How on earth did she know I was in the furniture business!"

Like Cole Porter, the Duke and Duchess of Windsor also lived in The Waldorf Towers—among the exclusive upper floors of the hotel from the 28th to the 42nd floors. The Duke loved pug dogs and one evening he was walking his two dogs when he met one of the hotel employees. They started talking about their mutual interest in pugs when the employee suddenly realized he was talking to none other than the Duke of Windsor. He gasped, "Your Royal Highness!" Whereupon, the Duke, gently rebuked him and said, "Forget about that. Let's just be two friends talking about dogs."

Harry Belafonte was one of the first singers to follow Lena Horne into the Empire Room of the Waldorf-Astoria. Today, Mr. Belefonte, who has become an international icon, would command the hotel's Presidential suite if it were available. In those early years, his room at the Waldorf was somewhat smaller.

"We were with Richard Conte and his wife. They took us up to Harry's room," recalled film producer and former New York agent Martin Jurow. "It was about as big as a large sofa, literally. A little tiny room. And Harry was very dramatic. He felt that he was going blind. He later had an eye test and found out he had a little glaucoma, that's all. And he was sure he was going to lose his eyesight. I thought to myself for years—'you see, you didn't lose your eyesight!'"

President George W. Bush regularly stays at the hotel, in the presidential suite, for meetings of the United Nations Security Council. During a recent stay of my own, a large South Korean delegation had booked many rooms in the Towers and I ended up staying in a lovely newly redecorated suite in the main hotel. Comedian Jerry Lewis wouldn't stay anywhere else, he told me.

"Ever since Dean Martin and I first appeared in New York I've stayed either at The Waldorf or The Plaza," Mr. Lewis explained during a wide-ranging interview I had with him for The New York *Sun* in the Bull and Bear restaurant in November 2002. He also said: "Next Labor Day I'll be back to doing the (Jerry Lewis Muscular Dystrophy) Telethon 24 hours 'til I die. There's no way I will ever stop." Last Labor Day, illness forced him to cut back to 13 hours.

Pain in his spine triggered by comedy pratfalls "finally got to the point where it was so severe I was ready to kill myself," he said. But "for the first time in 37 years I'm without pain" through the use of a "Medtronic" medical device implanted in his back.

"I had four years of grieving for Dean (that is, of course, Dean Martin, Lewis' longtime partner) I cannot even explain," but "when I sat down and started to write *The Martin and Lewis Story* the grieving stopped. When I'm writing the book I feel like Dean is in the room with me," he continued. "I'm getting this wonderful plethora of beats and rhythms. I'm not Shirley MacLaine and not talking about channeling. I deeply feel Dean's presence. The grieving has stopped."

Lewis and Martin began their legendary show business partnership in 1946 when Mr. Lewis was performing at the 500 Club in Atlantic City. One of the entertainers quit the show but on his way out suggested Dean, with whom he'd worked at the Glass Hat in New York, as a replacement.

While Peacock Alley, the hotel's multi-star gourmet restaurant was temporarily closed as have other top hotel restaurants in the wake of the terrorist attack on the World Trade Center, and the subsequent drop in overseas tourists, the overall quality of the Waldorf's restaurants, including Oscars, a moderately priced restaurant, exceeds that of other hotels, old and new. Incidentally, Waldorf executive chef John Dougherty has been at the hotel for a quarter century, long ago having learned his craft from the late Eugene Scanlan (the only chef in the hotel's history to become general manager).

The hotel's state-of-the-art technology, meanwhile, continues to be on a par with or even to exceed the highest international business and conference standards. For example, the Starlight Roof's direct worldwide satellite link eliminates the need for a separate satellite truck. And the list—from worldwide videoconference to microwave transmission—goes on and on. But despite what all the world has to offer in software and hardware, The Waldorf-Astoria remains an island of luxury and celebrity in the place that, as the late Frank Sinatra sung, is a "City That Never Sleeps."

Of course, things around this particular island have changed dramatically in some ways.

"I can remember growing up in the hotel and being able to see the activity, the ships and traffic, on both rivers, the Hudson and the East River, from our suite in the Waldorf Towers," Conrad Wangeman, the general manager of the New York Hilton, told me. But while some of the views from the upper floors of The Waldorf-Astoria may not be what they were in the 1950's, 1960's and even the 1960's, nothing can obscure the view of the hotel from within and without. The glow of "the greatest," as Conrad Hilton called it, has only grown brighter with every passing year.

Just as the builders and designers of New York hotels learned from the triumphs and mistakes of The Waldorf, which first opened in 1893, New York hotels built in and after 1904 learned something from the Bellevue-Stratford Hotel which had opened in Philadelphia that same year. Aside from its series of rusticated marble bay windows and balconies, ornate mansard roof and interior design—brimming with the latest creature comforts, which distinguished it from predecessors—the 'Grand Dame of Broad Street,' built by Mr. Boldt (based on everything he had learned from The Waldorf-Astoria), featured a number of ground-breaking engineering and service features. These included the latest pneumatic-interchange tube system for conveying written messages at great speed. The Loomis Manning Filter Company designed the water filtration system which gave tap water some of the qualities of bottled purified water.

But if Boldt tried in Philly to improve on the amenities of New York's Waldorf, the interior had many similarities. The interior of The Bellevue Stratford Hotel constantly asserts, as it was doubtless intended to, The Waldorf-Astoria, Roger S. Lucas says in his book, *The Bellevue-Stratford Hotel*. Yet, he continues, "in spite of its smaller dimension the ground floor of the Bellevue-Stratford gives the impression of being more spacious than The Waldorf-Astoria, because it had been built all at once and planned as one hotel, instead of being planned as two hotels like The Waldorf and Astoria hotels were."

In the last decade, Hilton Hotels has poured hundreds of millions of dollars into renovating and restoring the already resplendent public spaces of The Waldorf-Astoria, as well as suites and single rooms, building on a legacy that was rooted in Conrad Hilton's love of the grand hotel.

But even the millions spent in restoring The Waldorf-Astoria to its original grandeur could not purchase its intangible dedication to service, which also sets it apart from most other hotels. Courtesy, friendliness and practical adherence to the legendary adage that George Boldt, its first manager, coined—"the customer is always right"—have remained as much hallmarks of The Waldorf-Astoria as its distinct towers. In the last decade, the hotel and its upper towers, rising from the 28th to the 42nd floors, have been showered with accolade after accolade. *Official Hotel Guide* gives the Waldorf Towers its highest honor, the Superior Deluxe Top 99 Award. Adding to its worldwide recognition, this hotel within a hotel became the first Conrad Hotel in North America, joining 11 other hotels in Hilton's luxury hotel holdings in Europe, Asia and elsewhere. Contributing substantially to the luster of the hotel was the restoration, completed in 2001, of the famous Starlight Roof, which earned the hotel the Business Achievement Award of the Preservation League of New York.

Eric Long, the current vice-president and general manager of the hotel, deserves much credit for his stewardship of the restorations and many of the ideas he's had, like the executive meeting center. "Just the entertainment facet of room service, private in-suite dinner parties, weddings, etc., has exploded this year and will be up 80 percent. It's really a great story," said Long, as he sat in the executive suite of The Waldorf-Astoria several stories above Lexington Avenue.

And, to be sure, wherever I looked as my wife and I stayed in the hotel recently for the first time in several years—walking through the lobby exquisitely decorated by Ken Hurd, the Presidential Suite, the 1,645-square-foot Basildon Suite or the 4,229-square-foot Empire Room, so much laden with entertainment history—The Waldorf-Astoria glistened as it must have on the day it opened on October 1, 1931. It also seems to me that having lived briefly with my family in the hotel and closely observed it researching the first edition of my book, *The Waldorf-Astoria: America's Gilded Dream*, that it appears to be in the best shape its been in many years.

"It's in better shape than its ever been in," asserts Rick Hilton, Barron Hilton's son, who has lived in The Waldorf Towers with his wife Kathy and daughter Paris and Nikki for many years.

Attending dozens of black tie functions in the Grand Ballroom gives one only an inkling of the previous millions who have enjoyed dining and entertainment on the grandest of scales in this same space. Executive Chief John Dougherty, in fact, is in charge of one of the largest food and banquet operations in the world.

Calling the Waldorf a "city-within-a-city" has special meaning when one realizes that in the early 1930s a master plan for midtown Manhattan proposed creating four "anchors" that boxed midtown and each one of these was a city-within-a-city. Grand Central, on the South, was the first of the anchors; Rockefeller Center, the second, The Waldorf-Astoria was the third and the fourth was never built. (The New York Public Library is an anchor of sorts but not a city-within-a-city as the other three are.) All of them (including the library) have undergone magnificent restorations.

In *Weekend at the Waldorf*, starring Ginger Rogers and Walter Pidgeon, there's a wonderful scene with Rogers running across the terrace of a Waldorf Towers apartment and waving to a plane which Pigeon has just taken off in. And then the camera pans the skyline of midtown Manhattan. At the time you could see to New Jersey and Connecticut from the Towers when The Waldorf-Astoria was the tallest hotel in the world and little else blocking its vistas north, south, east and west. But, somehow, The Waldorf-Astoria seems to be even more storied, more glorious and more accommodating today than in those earlier years of passenger flight, when Cole Porter wrote, "You're the Top, You're the Waldorf Towers."

CHAPTER 13
SURVIVING THE 1930'S

As New York hotels gradually pulled out of the Depression with the rest of the country in the mid-1930's, it's interesting to take note of how different a place New York was then from now. For one thing, The Waldorf Towers dominated the skyline, along with the Chrysler Building and Empire State, affording views from some suites down to the Statue of Liberty. World travel, of course, was more leisurely, generally by ship, on the high seas. My friend, the late Jim Troy, who produced "The Nat King Cole Show" from Chicago, embarked with his mother on a trip around the globe in 1935. It took them "eight days to get from Honolulu to Yokohama by steamboat," Troy told me. "The China Clipper air service wouldn't be available until November of that year, and that would take five days from San Francisco to Manilla…If we liked a place or there was more to see than we thought, we just waited for the next boat."

Perhaps Frank Case of The Algonquin best described the effects of the dual blows of Prohibition and the Great Depression:

"Fourteen years of Prohibition, followed by the Depression, which had a longer run than *Tobacco Road*, left the hotel keeper wan and wasted. How did any survive? The answer is that most of us did not survive…It was not the loss of the liquor business that brought desolation to the big hotels. Perhaps they could have struggled on, but they lost their restaurant business as well."

After making a small fortune writing some "talkies," including *Up in Central Park*, as well as being a highly paid "consultant" on the screen version of his New York newspaper play *Gentlemen of the Press*, my father lived at the Essex House with his second wife, Broadway producer Jean

Dalrymple, in a suite on the 38ᵗʰ floor facing Central Park that rivaled in reality the glamorous movie sound stages. A bevy of stage and screen beauties streamed into the hotel suite every night, and on any given night, the author of the celebrated "Broadway After Dark" column for The New York *Sun* was trading fashionable insults of the day with Dorothy Parker, Alexander Woollcott or Miriam Hopkins, who at one time had been a girlfriend of my father's. When Jean Dalrymple complained that he sent a then big Broadway star a hundred orchids, he bought the entire stock of the Essex House florist and had it sent up to their suite.

First lady Eleanor Roosevelt maintained a suite of rooms at the Essex House as did Rudolph Bing, former head of the Metropolitan Opera. Lily Pons, another long-time Essex House guest, shared her suite with a pet jaguar, who would freely roam through her rooms. Despite Miss Pons' claims that it was really "only a large pussycat," she eventually was persuaded to donate it to the Central Park Zoo.

Another frequent guest at the Essex House was Elsie Grossinger, who ran Grossinger's Resort in the Catskills. "Elsie Grossinger had a suite at the Essex House," Joel Pommerantz, who wrote a biography of the resort, told me. "She used to come to New York at least once a week. You could look out on the entire (Central) Park. She was on the 20th floor."

In fact, almost the entire movie *Big City Blues*, which was co-written by my father and came out in 1932, takes place in a suite on the 36ᵗʰ floor of a thinly-disguised Essex House. Bootleg liquor flows like proverbial water during a murder investigation by a tough-talking—out of the side of his mouth, naturally—detective. It starred Joan Blondell, who was a real blond bombshell in those years and featured a fresh-faced Humphrey Bogart who was trying to make it in Hollywood playing a cad. It would be several years before he would make it, however, as Duke Mantee in Robert Sherwood's *The Petrified Forest* opposite Bette Davis and Leslie Howard, who insisted that Bogart be in the movie after making a splash in the stage version in 1935.

In *Big City Blues*, the house detective sums up the situation in all hotels in the city during Prohibition when he laments, "I'd like to go into a New York hotel room just once and not find a gin (party) going on."

But there are also some rhapsodic odes to New York in the movie, as when Blondell tells her new friend, who has just come in from Indiana, "You know, Bud, I envy you terribly. Your first day in New York. The lights, the theaters, the millions of people, thrills and fun. Enjoy it, Bud. It will never be like it is now."

In some ways the 30's are still with us, as are the 1900's, and the WWII era and, you name it. The people and the property of New York remain a constant. Hoteliers really only give the old places a facelift every now and then. For instance, Architects Gary Handel and Associates reduced by more than half the number of guest rooms in the former 700-room Emery Roth-designed St. Moritz to produce the new Ritz-Carlton New York, which opened in 2003. Interior designer Frank Nicholson, who installed 21 original Samuel Halpert paintings in the new Ritz-Carlton lobby, gave it a distinct residential feeling. Artist Halpert is perhaps best known for his 1919 rendition of the Flatiron Building on 23rd Street, once the tallest building in the world (and still the flattest).

CHAPTER 14
THE MUSIC MAKERS

New York City's hotels have long throbbed with great music, and great musicians. Cole Porter lived lavishly in The Waldorf Towers but was fond of attending parties at the Essex House and The Pierre. He composed many of his most beloved songs on his grand piano in Suite 33A, including "Night and Day" and "You're the Top," which refers to the Waldorf Towers. Paul McCartney used to register at the Plaza as a ruse to avoid adoring fans but he actually stayed at The Stanhope. Musical comedy writer Alan Jay Lerner wrote "I Could Have Danced All Night" and other hit songs from *My Fair Lady* in all-night writing stints at The Algonquin. He met his most famous collaborator, Frederic Lowe, at the Lambs Club, a hotel-like club designed by Stanford White on West 44th Street near Times Square.

One great hotel that didn't quite make it deserves a mention here. Thirty blocks to the south of The Carlyle lay The Ritz-Carlton, which was razed in 1951 to make room for an office building. The Ritz held a special place in Artist and writer Ludwig Bemelmans' heart because this had been the hotel he patterned on his *Hotel Splendide*, perhaps his most famous book, after the "Madelaine" series.

Built in 1910, the Ritz was the height of class, including the great European chef Escoffier (the same fellow for whom that lovely two-bedroom suite in the Pierre was named), who prepared epicurean delights on opening nights. News of the demolition of the historic Ritz, "shattered many people to whom demolition of the Ritz means more than the end of a Manhattan landmark," *The New York Times* reported on February 4, 1951.

Aside from its original Bemelmans' murals, there are prints and original works by Audubon, Redoute and Vertes which give The Carlyle a gallery flavor. A friend, the late Nick Racz, who had been an assistant manager at Waldorf Towers, had a private collection of Vertes, given to him by the artist himself. Racz, who was the living embodiment of the adage "the customer is always right," lived almost as large as his work. He and his late wife, Jeannie, lived in an enormous penthouse duplex in a pre-war building at 46th Street and Lexington Avenue.

Other hotels are themselves intentional works of art. The Summit Hotel, "dramatically reflected the emotional character of East midtown," notes Robert A.M. Stern and his co-authors in their book *1960*.

It's no accident that the late Bobby Short, the greatest cabaret performer of his generation, played almost exclusively at the Café Carlyle, along with other greats like Woody Allen, Barbara Cook and Eartha Kitt. Aside from the Café Carlyle, Feinstein's at the Regency and the Oak Room of the Algonquin Hotel are the top cabarets in the city. But it is the Café Carlyle that almost single-handedly carries the torch song of the long vanished heyday of New York nightlife, when the Plaza's Persian Room, the St. Regis Roof and the Waldorf-Astoria's Empire Room vied with each other for musical and social supremacy.

In an interview in the Rosewood Hotel house newsletter, Glenn Collins of *The New York Times* talked to Woody Allen about clarinet technique when his band played at The Carlyle. "I don't like to get too slick," he told Mr. Collins. "I drop songs when they seem to be arranged. Sometimes the best is when we play a song for the first time and we don't know it too well. Of course, the lack of technique makes it always a first time for me."

Even Allen's imperfect playing took some time getting used to the acoustics of the Café Carlyle. "We fell straight off but it took us a while to get used to the acoustics. It's so intimate."

When he started playing at the Café Carlyle on Monday nights in 1997 after having played regularly at Michael's Pub for years he had a tough act to follow in Bobby Short who had been at the Café Carlyle for nearly a quarter century.

Allen himself had spurned some of the biggest musical stars of his teens for the then more obscure New Orleans jazz sounds. "Other kids at school liked such vacuous tunes (as Sinatra sang)," Mr. Allen told Mr. Collins. "But New Orleans music was very beautiful to me. I bought one album. Then another. It was an adolescent obsession, like being involved with stamp collecting."

The appearance of all the stars at The Carlyle is a perplexing contradiction. Here you have one of the most sedate off-the-beaten-track kinds of hotels carrying on a tradition that was begun by the glitzier, decidedly more public hotels like the Waldorf-Astoria, The St. Regis and The Plaza and their premier music rooms like The Empire and Persian rooms. It's really only The Regency and The Algonquin which can boast some of the traditions of these great rooms of former glory. And The Carlyle's Café Carlyle. But the latter is where Mr. Allen has chosen to play his Indian Army clarinet, which he said cost "all of $49.99."

Call him one nice guy. Woody Allen, who apologized to jurors and even shook hands with Judge Ira Gammerman after the lawsuit with his former producer Jean Domanian was settled in 2002, once went out of his way to sign an autograph for one eight-year-old named Sydney. At the time, Allen was shooting his "Spring Project" movie in Manhattan's John Jay Park overlooking the East River.

"As we left the park, we saw Woody in the passenger side of the front seat of a black car with three other people. Sydney pointed to him. He saw her and waved. They all got out of the car and headed into the park." Sydney's mother told me. "Sydney ran after them with me tailing behind and said, 'Excuse me, Mr. Allen!' He stopped first and then the others stopped. Sydney handed him a piece of paper and pen and he said 'sure' and signed an autograph. Sydney and I both thanked him and he said 'sure, no problem.'"

Barbara Cook, another recent Café Carlyle headliner, told *Playbill* scribe Harry Haun that as time went on in her glorious singing career, acting played an ever more important role.

"When I first started out," she said, "I didn't give much thought to acting a song. That evolved. Now I think of it as living inside a song and singing my way out—inhabiting it, feeling it, and making it felt from my core to your core."

Incomparable jazz pianist Barbara Carroll was lunching on shrimp and chicken at Nirvana, the fabulously beautiful Indian restaurant high above Central Park South just steps west of The Plaza. After playing the piano and singing at Bemelmans' Bar at the Hotel Carlyle for the last 24 years she told me she was "getting back to my jazz roots…I'll be at Birdland…I'll be at the JVC Festival at the Sylvia and Danny Kaye Playhouse."

"I just want people to know that life goes on after The Carlyle...I began playing the piano at Bemelmans' Bar in 1978...I came for two weeks and they stretched it out. You create a clientele who keep coming back and bring other people who keep coming back and that's how one becomes established in a place like that...From Tom Selleck to Jack Lemmon." Lemmon, she said, would take Ms. Carroll's seat at the piano and play a few songs himself.

"People like Jack Nicholson, Jack Lemmon, Walter Matthau, Tom Cruise," she continued. "I am just thinking off the top of my head. Tom Selleck. Nicole Kidman. They all loved to stay at The Carlyle. Some came to Bemelmans' Bar. Some didn't. Jack Lemmon used to come in a lot. Jack Lemmon loved to play piano and he played well. He was one of the regulars. Warren Beatty. I suppose that reciting the names of people who used to go there is really name-dropping.

"It's so New York. People used to say, 'Oh, I just got off the plane from London or Paris or Los Angeles or Cincinnati and came here (to the Bemelmans' Bar) right away because people had very special feelings for that room. For one thing, Bemelmans' drawings made it unique. It was intimate; it was cozy. In Peter Sharp's days he was very careful to keep it special for the regular clientele.

"The guests were people who lived in the area. People from all over the country and from all over the world, really, who wanted to come in and have a drink and listen to the performance."

Over the years, Ms. Carroll has played not only bebop and all varieties of jazz, but also every conceivable kind of pop—from entertaining at top cabaret rooms like Bemelmans to appearing on Broadway in the Rodgers and Hammerstein classic *Me and Juliet*. One of her happiest memories of Bemelmans is the late Jack Lemmon staying late one night to take over her seat at the piano.

Robert Preston Tisch, who remembers going to the Persian Room of The Plaza and the Empire Room at The Waldorf-Astoria, co-created the most elegant nightclub of the late 20th and early 21st Century in Feinstein's at The Regency. The late Laurence Tisch and his brother, Robert, knew their hotels. They also built the Americana and the Summit, both designed by the late architect Morris Lapidus. Lapidus also designed the famous Fontainebleau Hotel in Miami Beach. Feinstein's at The Regency is the place where Rosemary Clooney took one of her final bows as a singer. Singer songwriter Kenny Rankin, who has played at Feinstein's, told me, "I have a locker room in LA but I'll always be from New York." His famous rendition of "Rose of Spanish Harlem," which he didn't write, was first sung out of love for his former wife, Yvonne.

Michael Feinstein, who was once Ira Gershwin's assistant, sells out when he himself plays at Feinstein's at the Regency as he did at a Society of Singers benefit in October, 2003.

Feinstein helped raise thousands of dollars for the Society of Singers, a charity that gives grants to singers in need of financial assistance. Between songs at Feinstein's at the Regency, Mr. Feinstein said it was he who was indebted to the audience for the opportunity to sing songs he rarely if ever sings. "It's a pleasure, truly, to sing for all of you," he told the audience that included former big-band singer Fran Warren, nostalgia radio personality Joe Franklin, and TV producer Sy Kravits, the father of pop/rock singer Lenny Kravits. "I have chosen some songs I don't have a chance to do that often because I thought if there was ever an erudite group, this is it!

"I also discovered that there are over 800 songs that were published by George Gershwin, and because of that it's always impossible to sing the ones I love or all that you love and that's why I'd like to take requests," he added. "Somebody Loves Me," someone shouted. "Somebody Loves You?" Mr. Feinstein joked rhetorically before doing one of the more well-known numbers of the evening.

I interviewed the late Rosemary Clooney in December 2000 when she was singing at Feinstein's and staying at the Surrey Hotel. In the interview, the internationally famous star, who celebrated her 50th year singing professionally in 1995, called family her biggest blessing. "I'm so grateful for my family. My children. My ten grandchildren and my husband, Dante. He's the love of my life," Ms. Clooney said. "But I've never quite forgiven Dante because he chose to be in the movie *Seven Brides for Seven Brothers* over *White Christmas*," Ms. Clooney joked. "He has on occasion sung with me in nightclub acts, but he would prefer to sing by himself because he likes to sing all of his songs in Italian!"

Ms. Clooney and Mr. DiPaolo, a former dancer and singer, married in 1997 after having been close friends for more than 20 years. Ms. Clooney was first married to the late stage and screen star José Ferrer, with whom she had five children. "I'll never forget one Christmas when Joe [Mr. Ferrer] was doing a play on Broadway. We had a suite at The Plaza; a Christmas tree from FAO Schwartz; a live tree that they had decorated. It was one of the nicest Christmases I ever had," she reminisced. Her career started when she sang duets with her sister Betty for WLW Radio in Cincinnati in 1945. Two years later, "The Clooney Sisters," as they were billed, made their debut at the famed Steel Pier in Atlantic City, NJ. Ms. Clooney became a star when she recorded her first single, "Come On-a My House" in 1951, and it became a huge hit. She told me *White Christmas* costar Danny Kaye was a much better singer and actor than he was a dancer; she couldn't dance very well, either; and costar Vera-Ellen could dance but not sing, and her songs were dubbed. So it's little wonder why there were plenty of laughs from the audience at Feinstein's when she wryly concluded before showing a film clip: "So here you have a singer who can't dance and a dancer who can't sing!" Bing Crosby, of course, was the star of the movie as well as a great friend of Ms. Clooney's. I asked Mr. DiPaolo why Rosemary never married Bing and he answered with a laugh, "She liked me better!" It's true that Bing and Rosemary were never romantically involved (at least off screen). More importantly, Mr. DiPaolo never missed a live performance of his wife's.

At the Drama League's gala honoring Jerry Orbach at The Pierre, one of the original cast members of *The Fantasticks*, syndicated columnist Liz Smith was one of the hits of the evening. "I love everything about the theater," she told me. "And like all amateurs I'm a real ham." Later, on stage at The Pierre (in the Grand Ballroom), Broadway legend Chita Rivera told guests that she had "been having a painful life doing the tango with Antonio Bandaras (who was in a revival of *Nine* with her at the time.) Somebody's got to do it!"

Noel Coward's ever-popular song, "I've Been to a Marvelous Party" epitomizes The Stanhope Hotel and it's only fitting that the phenomenal Steve Ross, who sang there in the fall and winter, sang it. New York *Times* music critic Stephen Holden called The Stanhope the "perfect setting for a musician who appears to have been born in a tuxedo." The Stanhope was a favorite of Paul McCartney and Edward G. Robinson.

Opera singers were not limited to the Ansonia or Knickerbocker, although many of them preferred it. Even The Algonquin got into the act with the old Metropolitan Opera House just blocks away. Frank Case, the late owner and manager of The Algonquin, tells in his book *Tales of a Wayward Inn* of singer Olive Fremstand who stayed at The Algonquin when she was studying the role of Kundry in *Parsifal*. Case recalled, "She sent for me one day to say she had to sing for hours in preparation for the performance and feared she might be annoying others in the hotel. 'Yes, it's terribly annoying,' I told her; 'come out in the hall and I'll show you.' Three separate doors to three apartments were open and on a chair in each doorway sat a hotel guest having a grand time listening to his own private opera!

"When Elsie Janis was getting ready to appear in a musical show later to score a big hit on Broadway, a young man used to come in almost every day to play the piano for her and help her rehearse her songs. He was a nice, mannerly young fellow, to whom I would give a casual hello, neither polite nor rude, just casual, for he was no one in particular. Today when I read *Present Indicative* and learned that at that very time he was living in a borrowed flat in the Village, struggling with a gas stove, I wish I had been a little nicer to Noel Coward."

Architecture isn't the only thing that The Americana, now the New York Sheraton, had going for it. The hotel continued the tradition, begun by the Hotel Pennsylvania, Roosevelt, Waldorf-Astoria and others, of the big band era. In 1963, Frank Sinatra, Jr., who was born in California and got his early musical training on bandstands the world over, had his professional debut at the Americana Royal Box with the Tommy Dorsey Orchestra.

Frank Sinatra, Jr., carved out a career as a bandleader. I talked to him when he came to New York in the summer of 2003 to be the first star attraction of the Little Italy Summer Festival. He said he one day would like to bring his band to Broadway and misses his dad a great deal. Sinatra's father celebrated his 80th birthday at the Waldorf-Astoria.

Robert Lissauer, a music publisher for nearly half a century, got to know many of the big band leaders like Glenn Miller and Benny Goodman. Goodman played at the Waldorf-Astoria back in 1932 with headliner Russ Columbo, who was a rival of Bing Crosby's at the time.

One time Glenn Miller summoned Lissauer and told him he had made up his mind to enlist; he said he felt guilty about sitting out World War II playing music. Miller never did enlist but was lost aboard a plane that was crossing the English Channel. No one ever discovered exactly what happened—whether it went down in bad weather or was actually shot down.

Benny Goodman played the Waldorf-Astoria in 1932 with Russ Columbo singing with the band. A number of the hotels, including the Roosevelt, the Waldorf-Astoria and the McAlpin, featured big band broadcasts on the radio.

After playing with the Ben Pollack band in Chicago and Atlantic City, Goodman got his first New York exposure when the Pollack band was booked into the Park Central Hotel in 1928. In fact, according to James Lincoln Collier's *Benny Goodman and the Swing Era*, the Park Central became a hotter entertainment spot after gangster Arnold Rothstein was shot there.

"Bill McGuire played at the McAlpin and Charlie Long was at the New Yorker," Mr. Lissauer recalled. I asked Mr. Lissauer if he thought that Glenn Miller, who he became friends with, was the greatest of all the bandleaders. "It's hard to say," he said. "They all had such individuality. One time Miller asked him whether he thought a particular classical composition would sell more records, something which Miller himself thought, than a little ditty called "String of Pearls," which went on to become a mega-hit. Miller also confided he wanted Lissauer to start a record label for him but this and other hopes and dreams ended for the great bandleader when he died in that flight across the English Channel.

Ellsworth Statler, one of the country's pioneering hoteliers, coined the catch-phrase that has ever since guided the building and promotion of hotels: "Location, location, location," and no hotel has ever had a better location as far as transportation is concerned than the Hotel Pennsylvania opposite Pennsylvania Station. He opened it in 1919, with rooms "with a bath for a buck and a half." Glenn Miller, who played in the hotel's famed Rouge Room, also made it a cornerstone of big band history with his song "Pennsylvania-6-5000." But Count Basie, Duke Ellington and the Dorsey Brothers, also played at the Pennsylvania.

New York publicist Phil Leshin remembers staying at Harlem's famous Teresa Hotel, which the big band stars of the 1920s called their home away from home while playing the Apollo across 125th Street. "I was a bass player with the Buddy Rich band and I stayed there in the 1950s. It wasn't great at that time. It was OK. But I didn't want to go downtown." Mr. Leshin went on manage and do publicity for Lionel Hampton, who I interviewed several times thanks to him.

Ruby Dee, who starred in *A Raisin in the Sun* on Broadway and many other shows, remembers visiting the Hotel Teresa but never staying there as many black bandleaders had done. "I was there a lot—you had meetings there," Ms. Dee told me. "We lived not far away on 7th Avenue and 137th Street—what my mother called a 'good address.'" U.S. Representative Charles Rangel, speaking at the funeral for Lionel Hampton at the Riverside Cathedral in 2002 said that his stint working behind the front desk of the Hotel Teresa gave him the idea to tell people he was a close friend of Duke Ellington and other black bandleaders who frequented the hotel.

Joe Franklin was a surprise guest at Danny Stiles' 80th birthday party on aMonday night in December at John's Pizzeria restaurant on West 44th Street.

"Over the years, I interviewed Bing Crosby, Eddie Cantor and one of my all-time favorites is Danny Stiles," Mr. Franklin told Mr. Stiles and hundreds of well-wishers after the two radio legends hugged each other warmly.

"It's nice to be recognized but it's more important to be nice," Mr. Stiles replied.

"Tomorrow marks 56 years as a radio broadcast host," Mr. Stiles told me that night. "I love it now more than ever. They'll probably have to carry me away from the studio when I'm on the air."

Mr. Stiles is the host of "Big Band Sounds" each Saturday evening from 8-10 P.M. on WNYC (820AM) in New York. He also does late night radio shows on WNSW and WPAT. He began his radio career in New York on December 2, 1947, over WHBI and is in the tradition of such on-air greats as Martin Block ("Make Believe Ballroom"), William B. Williams, Lonny Star and Al Collins on WNEW. He features such artists as Sophie Tucker, Harry ("Mr. Broadway") Richman, Guy Lombardo, Dinah Washington, Louis Prima, Xavier Cugat, Buddy Clark, Bing Crosby, The Boswell Sisters, and Shirley Temple. Mr. Stiles' biggest regret about the Big Bands of decades earlier is he couldn't afford to see them live at The Waldorf and other hotels.

"One time, I established a record by representing four bands in New York City at the same time," the late Gary Stevens told me. "There was Johnny Long at The New Yorker Hotel, Bobby Sherwood at The Lincoln Hotel, Louie Prima at The Strand Theatre and Tony Pastor at The Paramount. I was racing around all day."

Mr. Stevens represented Mel Torme when he at The St. Regis. "He had several records going for him then," Mr. Stevens said. "His manager, who is still a good friend of mine, hired me as his publicist and I stayed on and off with Mel for four years."

"He was a hard guy to handle because he had a high opinion of himself, justifiably, I guess, but he was very bossy. When I started with him I had to lay the rules down, saying, 'Look Mel, I know who you are and you may be one of the greatest singers of all time, but I'm not a member of your fan club, I'm just telling you how I feel. I don't want any problems. I know you're a tough guy but I don't want you ordering me around. If you want to work together, I'll do the best I can for you.' And from that point we had a good working relationship, he respected me. But he was tough."

"I played the Pioneer Room at the Hotel Pennsylvania," band leader and former Johnny Carson "Tonight Show" regular Skitch Henderson told me." That's where I started in 1946. I thought it was the way to fame but the band business was over. Bing Crosby and an attorney by the name of Arnold Grant each lent me $700. That's how I started the band. The war was just on. It was called 'Skitch Henderson and His Orchestra' ... The Hotel Pennsylvania was then still popular. It was really a place you could go dance—and subways were a dime!"

In the 1930s and 1940s pretty much "all the hotels had bands," explains Vince Giordano, whose band, Vince Giordano and the Nighthawks, plays music of the 1920s at Charlie O's Time Square Grill. Mr. Giordano has also recorded the music for five Woody Allen films.

"I played piano at the Warwick Hotel but that wasn't the start of it," Cy Coleman, the Broadway composer of a dozen hit musicals, told me. "It was a place called the Little Club. It was when they had all those smart little spots in the 50s, and I played the Warwick Hotel, too. I played the Shelburn Hotel. I played the Sherry-Netherland. I was starting to write (music). The Sherry-Netherland, they gave me a huge party. We had half of the society of New York there. It was wonderful. We've lost a great deal of the nightlife of New York. It was really sensational. It was wonderful when you'd go to one club to another. You'd hear me, you could hear Marian McFarlane, you could hear Bobby Short. Just so many people. You can still hear a lot of them but it just changed—the whole atmosphere. I wish it would come back. Now, people go home and watch television and do other things."

I believe I had one of the last interviews with Broadway composer Cy Coleman who died just before Thanksgiving, 2004, at age 75, and whose contributions to pop music include "Witchcraft," "The Best Is Yet to Come," "Hey There Good Times," "I'm a Brass Band" and dozens of others.

Going to a night club in a hotel used to be a "special event" for his parents, says theater impresario Scott Seigel. "They were middle-class people living in New Jersey. For them it was a special event. An anniversary or a birthday. My father is still living and he's very pleased I get to experience that on a regular basis at Feinstein's at the Regency and other places he can only do from time to time."

Listening to great music in a great New York hotel has long been a memorable event for millions of people. Luckily for all of us, at intimate rooms all around the city, it still can be.

CHAPTER 15
HOTEL PEOPLE ON PARADE

Things that happen in hotels often make news, from jewel heists to movie junkets and press conferences. But rarely do hotels go out of their way to generate news, other than routine press releases. This was not the case at The Plaza, which, as part of its 75th anniversary celebrations, sponsored a series of revealing discussions with business and art leaders of the day.

Former Plaza manager Philip Hughes inaugurated the interviews with high profile business people and celebrities. Here's a sampling, Spring 1983:

Back in 1940, a 25-year-old Harvard graduate and newlywed took his first job: as secretary to the late (and much-loved) Mayor of New York, Fiorello La Guardia.

Forty-three years later, David Rockefeller was still, as he put it in 1983, "immersed in New York City." As chairman and prime mover behind the New York City Partnership, Inc. Rockefeller helped bring together citywide business, government and community interests to help solve some of New York's most pressing problems.

In his Rockefeller Center office, Rockefeller welcomed The Plaza's managing director, Philip Hughes, for a brief discussion of the Partnership's accomplishments and plans. The former head of the Chase Manhattan Bank and then chairman of at least six other major business, civic, charitable and cultural organizations began by explaining how he came to head the Partnership.

"In 1979 I was asked by some of the directors of the Economic Development Council of New York City (EDC) and of the New York Chamber of Commerce and Industry if I would become chairman of both, to help them work more closely together.

"I said I'd be glad to, providing that the two organizations could be used as a kind of base on which to build a broader, truly citywide organization. The Chamber, after 200 years, no longer represented the entire city. The other boroughs had developed their own chambers and New York's basically represented only Manhattan.

"The EDC was also largely supported by Manhattan interests. So it seemed to me that if we wanted to get business in New York to speak out on major issues with a single voice, we had to have something bigger. And since these two groups had the support of leading banks, financial institutions and corporations, I thought they would be a good base on which to build."

Members from all of New York's business organizations were invited to join with EDC and Chamber board members into a "partnership." The group's board grew to 120 representatives from the business, community and ethnic groups of all five New York City boroughs. They devoted themselves to aiding the city, gratis, coordinating their own resources with those of government and organized labor.

The Partnership's success as of the 1980's was astonishing, considering the tendency of most diverse groups to get bogged down in bureaucracies. "Youth employment was one of the first issues we decided to concentrate on," Rockefeller explained. From 1981 to 1983 the Partnership has helped create 35,000 summer jobs for disadvantaged youth.

How was it done? The Partnership's task force of volunteers contacted thousands of New York City firms to ask for jobs. Each year the task force was headed by representatives of a different company: New York Telephone the first year, Citicorp the second, and Philip Morris.

Rockefeller loved to travel and sail. Mr. Hughes, naturally, wanted to know some of Rockefeller's favorite hotels. These include Claridge's in London, the Plaza Athenee in Paris, and the Mauna Kea on the Big Island in Hawaii, developed by Rockefeller's brother Laurence. "I can mention it because some one else owns it now," Rockefeller laughed. "Otherwise, I wouldn't have wanted to toot the family horn."

There used to be a restaurant in the San Carlos Hotel called Big Julie's. And Big Julie was not big. He was a little guy. One day he found a homeless young lady in Central Park and brought her back to his suite at the San Carlos where he lived above his restaurant.

"I assume it was romantic," one former San Carlos employee told me. "At the beginning, I believe he was more of a father figure. She was very young, maybe 18 or so and had been living in the streets. He basically got her cleaned up and before you knew it she was a model with a modeling agency. But only after he bankrolled her modeling career. I used to chat with her. She was beautiful. She used to say, 'Imagine what would have happened if this guy hadn't found me in Central Park?' She was a runaway from somewhere in the Midwest. And she was living at the San Carlos, a beautiful hotel."

The San Carlos, incidentally, also got a major renovation in 2003 at a cost of some $22 million.

Before the Empire Hotel on Broadway across from Lincoln Center was renovated by Metromedia a number of longtime guests used to sit in the lobby on a big round couch. "It was like watching birds sitting on a branch," a former employee told me. "There was a pecking order. All these people had their spots on the couch. They all had their own places. And then if a transient guest would come in and attempt to sit down anywhere on this couch, the old people would say, 'What are you doing? You don't belong here. This is our seat.' But eventually management got so sick and tired of them monopolizing the couch that it was removed."

The Empire also had other weekly or monthly guests who had made a name for themselves. For example, Barbara Cook lived there in the 1970's when she was beginning to make the transition from Broadway to the top ranks of cabaret. "I found out who she was; she was 'Marion, the Librarian.' She played the role in *The Music Man* in the 1950's," this same former employee told me. "So I started talking with her. That was a transition period for her. Musicals were no longer what they had been when she was in *The Music Man.* "

Ms. Cook has since gone on to become a great solo performer like Judy Garland and Liza Minnelli and moved to Riverside Drive. When the former employee got Ms. Cook to permit a rock groupie to stay in her room while Ms. Cook was out-of-town for several weeks, management found out about it and had him fired. Unrepentant, he told me that the Empire "wasn't a great hotel in those days but you met really fascinating people. Today, you don't have residential hotels for those types of people— and some of them trying to get their careers restarted."

Over the years, a lot of tourists and leisure travelers never realized that many old hotels had long-term residents that were sometimes literally hidden away from view of the tourists. The tourists paid more for their rooms, but those parts of the hotel were more likely to be renovated than the apartments. These hotels included what is now called the Melrose, which was built in 1927, as the Barbizon Hotel for Women, and The Empire and others. Some had lived at these hotels for 50 years and were paying only $100 a month.

"Some of these people who lived in these hotels, which were beautiful, gracious hotels in their heyday and have seen better days, will talk about them as if it was yesterday," one hotelier said. "In hotels like the old Barbizon Hotel for Women, there was what people in the industry called 'a tale of two cities' in the hotel even after it was initially renovated. On several floors, walls were erected between the rooms occupied by these long-term residents and transient guests, with the hallways and rooms of the residents remaining as they had been for years in sharp contrast to the renovated portions. If you were to go down the hallway and open the door to where the residents were living it was dingy with shared bathrooms."

"The George Washington. Talk about a cast of characters!" exclaimed a former manager of the George Washington Hotel on Lexington Avenue and 23rd Street which has since been converted into student housing. "The cast of *One Mo' Time* stayed at the George Washington. After the show was over they'd have to unwind...We would have a lot of fun. They talked about how the show went and how the audience reacted...There was also an exotic dancer who lived there and a famous female impersonator...Obviously, not your mainstream jobs."

Built in the 1920's the George Washington had some 600 rooms, most of which were small. The exotic dancer who lived there has also stayed at the Woodward Hotel on West 55th Street, where my late sister, actress Ruth Maitland and her family has also lived. Maitland had been in *Junior Miss* on Broadway. As an understudy for Ruby Keeler in a revival of *No, No, Nannette* in the 1970's, she subbed for the star for two weeks. Since many performers traveled so much it wasn't practical for them to have an apartment on a long-term lease.

This particular exotic dancer performed at the Ibis on East 50th Street across from the San Carlos Hotel. Prostitutes, on the other hand, almost never were permanent residents of hotels even though some were better dressed and more well behaved than some women guests.

"You kind of have a relationship with prostitutes because it's kind of part of the business—it always has been," explains one hotelier. "In first-class hotels, they know that as long as they are discreet, as long as they make a good appearance, as long as a guest escorts them from the lounge no one is going to have a problem with that."

Of course, ladies of the evening aren't the only class of people striving to go unrecognized in hotel lobbies. Celebrities try, but rarely succeed, to go incognito in their own ways. Paul Newman liked to go to concerts and the ballet at Lincoln Center but was loath to have a drink in the public restaurants and bars there during intermission. So, he'd run over to the bar in the Empire Hotel and hang out there. "A couple of women were seated a couple of seats away and they begged a waiter to ask Paul Newman for an autograph," one regular patron of the bar told me. "The waiter went over and said, 'Mr. Newman, I'm sorry to bother you, I know you like your privacy here but they'd like your autograph.' He said, 'No I don't sign autographs but why don't you buy them both drinks.'" And he handed the waiter money for the drinks.

Other celebrities seem to have gone out of their way to attract attention. Film star Nastassia Kinski let a room service waiter in when she was totally naked so many times that he finally complained to his boss and asked to be relieved of the assignment. "I'm married and have kids, it's embarrassing," he said. O.J. Simpson used to preen naked in front of a mirror while a room service waiter was arranging his order. While there was nothing overtly sexual about O.J.'s behavior, other than that he was naked, the room service waiter thought it was strange behavior to say the least.

One hotelier recalls when Judy Garland, who'd been staying at a small hotel on Manhattan's East Side and not paying her bills, was physically thrown out of the hotel. "She was literally sitting on the curb on her luggage and cursing out anyone who passed by," I was told. Eventually, a friend came and picked her up.

The late publicist, Gary Stevens, moved into the Belvedere Hotel west of Eight Avenue in 1938 where he paid a rate of $4 a day, and he split this with actor Leon Ames, who was his roommate at the time. Perhaps Stevens' funniest story involving New York hotels of this period is the day he ran into Broadway actor Ray Middleton, who was carrying a doctor's bag up to one of the rooms in the Barbizon Hotel for Women on East 63rd Street. Grace Kelly and many other actresses who went on to become big stars lived at the Barbizon because it was considered to be a safe and secure hotel. "I said, 'Hey, Ray, how are you doing?' He said, 'Shush, I'm doctor George Brown!' Men weren't permitted above the lobby in the hotel so there were many 'doctors' in the Barbizon Hospital!"

The Philip Morris commercial, "Call for Philip Morris," featuring a bellboy calling for Philip Morris, one of the most famous commercials in history, originated in the lobby of the Hotel New Yorker at 34th Street and Eight Avenue. An ad man, who'd been assigned the account, was sitting in the lobby reading a newspaper. "And a little fellow by the name of Johnny Roventini, who was the pageboy at the New Yorker Hotel and was 4 feet, nine inches tall, was calling, 'Call for Sam Jones!' and the idea just hit Bill Bilow, the ad man," Stevens told me shortly before he died in 2004. "Bill 'this is a good way to kick off (the ad campaign) for Philip Morris.' I don't know what Johnny was making. Maybe $15 a week, plus tips. He gave him five dollars and he said, 'Do me a favor, All day long pace up and down and page Philip Morris!' And that's how it happened. Philip Morris, when they went on national radio, used that theme for nine years. 'Call for Philip Morris!' And they used the little guy. He went from $15 to $200 a week. He left his job as a page boy and became a celebrity on radio." It was, you might say, a call above and beyond the ordinary.

CHAPTER 16

THE CENTURY'S
THIRD HOTEL BOOM

Like the Americana Hotel, developed by Laurence and Robert Preston Tisch, architect Morris Lapidus said the angles in the Summit Hotel were not just for "shock value." "It's more than design; it's for added strength, cushioning the full force of wind gusts," he said in his autobiography, *The Architecture of Joy*, published in 1979. More like today's eminently successful hotel impresario Ian Schrager, who creates as much mood as comfort, Mr. Lapidus stated that hotels were for a vacation away from home. "Who wants a homey feeling on vacation?" he asked in his book.

Stern, Thomas Mellions and David Fishman in their book *1960* explain "The Summit Hotel represented a watershed in the post war resuscitation of the city's hotel industry. It was also important to the architectural community, its unabashedly theatrical interpretation of the International Style Modernism hitting a nerve."

The Regency, built in the early 1960s by the Tisch family, was a throwback to the more demure apartment style hotels of the 1920s like The Lombardy and The Mayflower but it was soon nicknamed "Hollywood East" for all the high-profile stars and celebrities who stayed there. Unlike The Algonquin or Mayflower or Carlyle, high profile guests who stayed at The Regency preferred to be in the spotlight. This was carried a bit to the extreme with the McGuire Sisters. They would come back from an engagement and as soon as they got out of their limo the evening manager would pop a McGuire Sisters tape into the hotel's lobby sound system. It was an isolated throwback of sorts to what famous Times Square eateries like Rector's or Shanley's used to do—but with their own live orchestras—when the star of that day used to come in after their Broadway shows. Well, the McGuire Sisters would start singing in harmony to the album and everyone in the lobby would join in.

Barbra Streisand, Sylvester Stallone, Goldie Hawn and, even Frank Sinatra, after he had given up his permanent suite at The Waldorf Towers in the early 1990s, stayed at The Regency.

Perhaps the biggest and zaniest robbery in the history of New York City hotels took place at The Regency in the early 1990s. Five machine gun-carrying thieves got more than a million dollars in jewelry.

"Five guys had already checked into the hotel," recalls Robert Shanley, who was the night auditor at the time of the robbery. "The security officer was most likely asleep, and my feeling is it was just as well—he could have been killed. They showed up with a bag of safe deposit keys and they had me get down on my hands and knees and start opening them. I said to myself, 'Oh, my God, it looks like they have every key from every safe in the hotel and it's an inside job.' But none of the keys would open any of the boxes. One guy was prodding a gun in the back of my head and saying, 'Get them open!' And I said, 'Look, these safes are not going to open.' And it was clear after trying five or six or ten of them that the keys were no good."

The thieves, however, were very well prepared. They brought sledge-hammers as a backup and they proceeded to whack away at the safe deposit boxes. (They had previously already deactivated the alarm system which was located in the telephone room in the basement.) Hotel guests, who were still straggling in, were put in the ballroom and kept watch over by one of the machine gun-toting thieves.

"Mickey Mantle's box was broken into, Cyd Charisse's box was broken into," Mr. Shanley recounted. "They gave me names of people who had boxes so they even knew who lived in the hotel. They opened about 35 to 40 safes and the noise from the sledgehammers started waking up some of the guests on the second floor. All the other employees were locked up in the ballroom and I was their designated hostage and I had to answer the phones. Guests were calling down and saying, 'What is going on down there?' And I said, with this gun at the back of my head, 'We had a major pipe break and we're doing emergency repairs and if you want to have water in the morning it has to continue.'"

To top it all off, a famous older woman sculptor who lived in the hotel at the time and had dementia came down and "she actually said to the thieves, 'Would you like to join me for breakfast?' And these guys were looking at her as if saying to themselves, 'Is this woman for real. We're holding these guns.' And I'm saying to myself, 'Oh, God, this is all I need!' Actually, the thieves handled it very well. They knew that she was not all there."

When the thieves left the ringleader asked for his registration card so his identity could not be traced. The hotel later found a record of his credit card in the computer but it had been stolen and the robbery has yet to be solved.

Because New York Yankees' owner George Steinbrenner lived at The Regency he had apartments for Mickey Mantle and Billy Martin there as well. Mantle was still with the Yankees organization doing promotion for it even though he had retired as a player years earlier. Mantle and Martin had regular seats at the bar, which in the early 1990s at any rate, was not all that popular. Certainly it took a back seat to the well-attended "power breakfasts" in the dining room of The Regency. But Mantle and Martin liked the fact that they had the bar virtually to themselves. And they proceeded to get drunk. "Mantle was the 'bad drunk' and Martin was the 'good drunk'" is the way one employee at the time called them. "Everyone thought Billy Martin was a monster because of the fights they had read about in the papers," this source said. "He used to hold court in the lobby and was a very friendly guy. He was very affable, very approachable. The more he drank the friendlier he got. Mantle, on the other hand, you didn't dare go near him when he was drunk; he could be very nasty."

One time a young boy of nine or ten years old was waiting out in the pouring rain to get an autograph from Mantle and he came in soaking wet and asked the former Yankee slugger to sign a baseball and Mantle was really very gruff to him and refused to do it. Whereupon Billy Martin's wife went over to Mantle and started yelling at him, saying, "You get out there and give him an autograph!" Mantle, very drunk, very sheepishly went outside and gave him an autograph.

The bar has since been taken out and replaced by a "living room" area for drinks and light meals similar to that in The Algonquin. A sidelight to Mantle's stays at The Regency was that he would be delivered cartons of new baseballs to his room and he would be up there for hours signing them.

Late actor Richard Harris, who starred in the movie version of the stage musical *Camelot*, stayed at The Regency around the time he was in a touring stage revival of the show. Often disheveled and looking more like a bag man than the famous actor he was, one night the night porter refused to let him into the hotel, not recognizing him as one of its distinguished guests. Harris proceeded to go to the median on Park Avenue and climb under a bench that was there and go to sleep. In the morning, the day doorman recognized who it was sleeping under the bench and Harris was whisked into the hotel.

"Sometimes he'd be humming and singing 'Camelot' and looking like a real character," a former employee told me. "He most always paid in cash and sometimes a check. Never a credit card. Room service kept a special container of oatmeal and had it labeled, 'For Richard Harris only.' He used to drive the chefs and the room service people crazy because he'd often send things back because he wasn't happy with something he ordered."

The actor certainly was a man of extremes when it came to paying his bills. He carried cash in a black satchel and would stack up $10 and $20 dollar bills in front of the front desk clerk to pay a bill that came to thousands of dollars.

Harris also loved staying at the Surrey Hotel on 76th Street between Madison and Fifth Avenue. "He had a closet locked up with his stuff in a suite. So he had it always available when he came here," Surrey manager Chester Deptula told me. "Rosemary Clooney would stay here and I went to her shows and had dinner with her. My little kids didn't know who she was until they saw *White Christmas* on TV. We had the first anniversary dinner for Rosemary at Patsy's last year which was attended by a lot of her friends."

I briefly got the chance to work behind the front desk of the Surrey Hotel on East 76th Street and found it was much more difficult than it looked. For one thing, you can't afford to let down your guard. You always must be ready and willing to help guests either in person or on the phone. "You can't be nice for three hours of an eight-hour shift and then tell the guest to, in effect, 'do it themselves,'" explained Robert Shanley, Chairman of the New York Food and Hotel Management School.

Sinatra also once showed up at The Regency very late one night after what appeared to have been an all-night drinking spree and walked smack into the hotel's glass front door. He was also without a bodyguard or escort, which seemed all the more unusual to those on duty in the lobby at the time. It was like he was still going through the rituals of the "Rat Pack" even though three members of the infamous drinking and carousing team had died.

Robert Preston Tisch, chairman of the board of the Loews Corporation, with assets in 2003 of more than $70 billion, and his late brother Laurence, purchased their first hotel in Lakewood, New Jersey before they purchased the controlling interest in Loews Theatres, Inc., theater chain in 1959 which became the foundation of the Loews Corporation today. The company became a pioneer in New York's hotel building boom in the 1960's.

"The first hotel we opened was July 31, 1961," Mr. Tisch told me in an interview in his Madison Avenue office. "This was the Summit Hotel on 51st Street and Lexington Avenue which was the site of the old Loew's Lexington Theatre. And then in December 1961 we opened the Howard Johnson Motor Lodge on 8th Avenue and 52nd Street. We sold it. In June of 1962 we opened the Ramada Inn on 8th Avenue and then in December 1962 we opened the Americana New York, which is now the Sheraton New York. Then on May 1, 1963 we opened The Regency, which we built. And then on December 16 of 1963 we built another motor inn. So we built six hotels in 26 months. By 1965 we took over the Warwick Hotel. In 1966, we took over the Drake Hotel. We had eight hotels in New York at one time. We built six and we acquired two. And kept them for seven or eight years and then started to sell some of them off. At one time we had 6,000 rooms in the city of New York."

This building spree caused quite a stir in real estate circles at the time but not as much as the actual design of two of the hotels, the Summit and the Americana New York, both of which were curved and designed by Morris Lapidus. "Morris didn't get the acclaim he deserved, and in my opinion, he was entitled to. Morris died seven or eight years ago. Only in the last 10 years of his life was he recognized as a great architect. He did the Fontainbleau, Eden Rock and the Americana (Bal Harbour) in 1955-56.

"We went there and saw the Fontainbleau and we started to build our hotel, (the Americana, Bal Harbour, now the Sheraton, Bal Harbour) right after the Fontainbleau opened. Morris was ahead of his time. That was a lot of his problem. Morris was a good architect who got a goodly amount of rooms out of each building."

"Ourselves and our people, we worked very quickly. I think we built before Morris filed the plans!" Mr. Tisch continued. Mr. Tisch started the "power breakfasts" at the Regency in 1976 during the depths of the city's fiscal crisis and they have been a huge success ever since. "The Regency always runs a little better than the industry in general. It's picked up very, very well since the decline a couple years ago."

George Steinbrenner is a regular at the power breakfasts and Mr. Tisch sees him all the time but doesn't try and give him advice on how to run the Yankees. "I talk to him a lot but that's not my job!" he said. "The hotel industry is still glamorous in New York and responsible for bringing in a lot of people to the city. Foreign tourists are coming back (since 9/11). At The Regency, you hear more foreign languages than you did a year ago. Now with the dollar so cheap compared to a lot of other currencies they will come back quicker. By the summer, we shall have a goodly number of foreign tourists."

"It's always good to be back at the Regency," singer Steve Tyrell told an opening night audience in January 2004. He then sang a song by Ira Gershwin and Vernon Duke which he said he'd slightly altered the lyrics to. An original line in the song was "I've been consulted by Franklin D. (Roosevelt) and even Garbo had me to tea." But in 1998 he changed it to "I've been consulted by President C (Clinton) and even Diana had me to tea." "She was beautiful; she was English—and that worked for me," he said.

The 1980's ushered in an era of unprecedented hotel renovation, which continued until the turn-of-the 21st Century with the overhaul of what had become single room occupancy hotels and the new Ritz-Carlton rising from the skeleton of the old St. Moritz. Some of these, to be sure, had started their lives as bachelor quarters.

New hotel construction, which had virtually stopped in the 1960's, began anew. The magnificent I.M. Pei-designed Four Seasons Hotel on East 57th Street is the most striking example of the new hotels that opened in the 1990's. Others blended old world charm with new construction and amenities. The New York Palace, originally called the Helmsley Palace and named after the late real estate mogul Harry Helmsley, opened in 1980. The Palace's lower floors are comprised of the restored 1882 Villard House, above which rises a 55-story tower. Formerly housing Le Cirque, perhaps New York's most celebrated restaurant, the Villard section of the hotel also includes the glorious Gold or music room, which would have been at home in Versailles, with its gilded carved mahogany and John LaFarge murals. Originally designed by McKim, Mead & White, the firm headed by Stanford White, the Villard Houses looks like a series of separate brownstone mansions. Patterned after the Palazzo della Cancellaria in Rome, it was built by Henry Villard, a prominent New York financier, and was only a block from the somewhat more magnificent Vanderbilt mansions on Fifth Avenue. Emery Roth & Sons designed the bronze and glass tower above the Villard House. During the restoration of the Villard House the courtyard facing Madison Avenue was redesigned with stones from several 15th century Italian cathedrals. One of the hotel's most striking features is its red Verma marble fireplace designed by Augustus Saint-Gardens and festooned with carved figures of Joy and Hospitality and flanked by fountains sporting marble dolphins.

The most famous occupant of the historic Villard Houses in the Palace Hotel was Sirio Maccioni's "Le Cirque 2000" restaurant, which opened in 1997 and announced it was closing seven years later. Mr. Maccioni was lured to the Palace in part by Richard Cotter, the hotel's manager, who'd already had a distinguished career in the hotel industry at The Waldorf-Astoria. But Mr. Cotter's departure, coupled with higher wages he was forced to pay employees who were members of Local 6 of the Bartenders and Club Employees Union, contributed to Mr. Maccioni's decision to move elsewhere. Since originally opening in 1974 in the Mayfair Hotel on East 65th Street, Le Cirque has hosted a plethora of "A" list celebrities that have included Nancy and Ronald Reagan, Frank Sinatra, Princess Grace, Rudy Giuliani and Diana Ross.

There are many newer grand hotels but few that bend into their historic surroundings as much as the TriBeCa Grand in TriBeCa at 2 Sixth Avenue. Leonard Stern, the billionaire chairman of the Hartz Group, built the Soho Grand in 1996 and the triangular $65 million TriBeCa Grand, with its cavernous atrium, five years later. "The goal was to make the TriBeCa Grand fit in so well with the area that it would seem as if it had always been there," Leonard's son, Emanuel, told me.

"Frankly, this plot was offered three years before I bought it at half the price and I said, Ah, forget it," Leonard Stern explained. "It was a terrible mistake. When I was re-offered it, I decided not to make a decision from my office but to come down and I called Manny and we immediately decided to buy it, realizing that we could have a freestanding hotel in Manhattan in an historic district. Then Manny and I discussed what we wanted out of it and I said, 'Manny, I want to be the architect.'"

"We did not want a building that stood out," Emanuel Stern said. "We wanted to be a good brick neighbor. One thing that is unique, not only for the TriBeCa Grand but for the city in general is that the entire main floor of the atrium for the Church lounge is a combination cocktail lounge and full-service restaurant where food or liquor or other beverages can be ordered 24-hours a day."

Leonard Stern takes credit for the atrium concept. "The idea for the atrium came to me when I was out in Bridgehampton. I had had two drinks. I was sitting looking over the balcony at the ocean and all of a sudden, I said, 'Ah, triangle! We'll make an atrium out of it.' That's how it happened. By the way, it was white wine so it wasn't that powerful!"

Perhaps only Cole Porter, the composer of "Night and Day" and "You're the Top" who lived at The Waldorf Towers, could have done justice to a song to herald the opening of the $260 million Mandarin Oriental Hotel on December 1, 2003.

Billy Joel sang four numbers, including his "New York State of Mind," to the crowd of more than 600 stars, celebrities, social, civic and business leaders who gathered in the hotel, located on the 35th to 54th floors of the new Time Warner headquarters on Columbus Circle. Guests included The Earl of Lichfield, I.M. Pei, Gina Lollobrigida, Leroy Neiman, Audrey Quock (the *Sports Illustrated* swimsuit issue model), Neil Sedaka, Catherine, Sabrina and Moira Forbes and dozens of others. Dr. Ruth, one of the guests, put the opening in this perspective: "I feel wonderful that we have the opening of a new hotel after '9/11.' The message is a very positive one for New York."

"This is such a unique hotel," said Catherine Forbes, the granddaughter of the late Malcolm Forbes. "And it's so exciting to see this kind of development on the Upper West Side."

"I'm going to sleep here tonight but then I have to go back home like Cinderella," film star Isabella Rossellini told me on a recent stay at the Mandarin Oriental Hotel on the eve of making her stage debut in a Terrence McNally play off-Broadway. "So I think I'll come here to the restaurants and the spa. I would love to live in a hotel but I don't think my employer will give me the money. I used to live on the east side and I used to like the Mark Hotel, which is also part of Mandarin. And Irene Selznick used to live at The Pierre Hotel, my mom's best friend. I haven't been in The Pierre for a long time but they had fantastic apartments.

"If they would ever do anything about my mother it should be about the years of the greatest success she had in her 30s," Ms. Rossellini said, about the possibility of a movie or play about her mother, late screen star Ingrid Bergman. Would Ms. Rossellini ever consider playing her mother? "I'm 50 so I'm too old!"

Joseph E. Spinnato, president of the Hotel Association of New York City (HANYC) said in a special magazine supplement marking the 125th anniversary for the HANYC in 2003 that he is "Optimistic for the (New York) Hotel industry because one thing I've learned in 15 years is the universal appeal of New York as a destination. The vast majority of people in this country, perhaps the world, want to come to it."

CHAPTER 17

SUMMING UP

To me, someone whose family has lived at The Plaza, Waldorf-Astoria, Algonquin and other hotels from the 1920s to the '60s, one of the best parts of New York hotels is you don't need a king's ransom to have a drink or tea there however much it now costs to have a room or suite. For example, a "light afternoon tea" in the posh Rotunda restaurant at The Pierre Hotel at Fifth Avenue and 61st Street is $29. Drinks at the Ritz-Carlton on Central Park South or the New York Palace, set within and above the 19th century Villard House on Madison Avenue between 50th and 51st Street are a more affordable fraction of the room rates.

Not the same can be said of the nightlife at some of New York's better known hotels such as The Carlyle and The Regency. The cover charge, not including dinner, for seeing Woody Allen and his band at the Cafe Carlyle on Monday nights is $80, while it was a whopping $90 to see the legendary crooner Bobby Short other nights. (These prices, comparable to Broadway ticket prices, don't include drinks or food.) The covers at Feinstein's at the Regency and the Algonquin's Oak Room are less. It was $55 for both the cover and drinks to see Barbara Carroll in her 8 p.m. Sunday night show at the Algonquin, where she performed songs of Cole Porter, George Gershwin and Stephen Sondheim.

If music charges vary, actual hotel costs are even more wide-ranging. A room at The Plaza on Central Park was more than $500 a night while a plethora of New York City "inns"—from the Marriott Marquis in Times Square to the 47-room Hotel 41 on West 41st Street, literally next door to where the musical *Rent* is playing, to the Hotel Pennsylvania where the late Glenn Miller once made big band history—are available even without using Priceline.com or Hotels.com for several hundred dollars less. In fact, the Pennsylvania, the Milford Plaza in Times Square, the Salisbury on West 57th Street are all in the "moderate" range. I recommend picking up a hotel guide, such as Michelin's New York City "Must Sees" guide, Gerry Frank's *Where To Find It, Buy It, Eat It In New York*, or Zagat's Hotel Guide for general price variations. They include many both north and south of Manhattan's midtown area, such as the 150-room Gershwin on East 27th Street and Wolcott Hotel on East 31st Street or the Excelsior on West 81st Street near the Museum of Natural History. At the same time, off the most beaten tracks don't necessarily mean bargain rates. The Mercer Hotel in Soho is expensive and, at least according to one guide it borders on "exorbitant."

You can, however, get more reasonably priced rooms that are not on Central Park, or not as large and ornate at the Pierre, Plaza, Essex House and many others if you do some comparative shopping. Since you often don't spend much time in your room anyway, this is one way of being in a hotel you prefer without paying top dollar. In the end, it's up to you. Only you can make a decision based on how much you want to spend and where. If it's modern ambiance—and money's not the object it usually is for most people—you can't beat the Four Seasons on East 57th Street. The W New York Hotel at 541 Lexington Avenue, on the other hand, is much more reasonably priced. If you want to stay in the very same room novelist Thomas Wolfe lived and wrote in you can do it at the Chelsea—and for not much more than tickets for a Broadway show. The buck, the choice, in "the city that never sleeps," as the song goes, stops and starts with you.

Socialite philanthropist Amanda Burden, who was honored in 2004 for her many contributions to the Cooper-Hewitt Museum, told me "there's an enormous expression of confidence in New York City. There are several factors. One is people want to build (hotels and others) here. And all the great architects of the city and the world are building here now because all of a sudden every sector of the public is saying, 'We want better. We want a building that's going to make our neighborhoods better. It's going to be beautiful.'"

In a number of ways the new and old hotels have now merged beautifully together in New York City. Today, for instance, the modernish Hilton is managed by Conrad Wangeman, the son of the Wangeman who ran The Waldorf-Astoria for many years. The current Mr. Wangeman, in other words, represents both the old and the new in New York hotel life. But when he talks about hotels, about his love for them, he doesn't talk about the money, of which of course there is at times a lot, or about the celebrities, of which at times there is too much, or even about the history, of which there certainly is a boatload. No, Mr. Wangeman cares most dearly about something else, and it is the essence, really, of hospitality, which is a hotelier's calling.

"From a sheer prestige point of view we're not maybe in line with The Waldorf," Mr. Wangeman continued in our interview that day. "We have a different market segment and Hilton believes it's the world's business meeting address and we sort of cater to that venue and that life. And I believe that Conrad Hilton believed that it was world peace for world travel which for this period of time is a wonderful concept. Hilton Hotels around the world facilitate that to this day. You know, we make a difference in so many people's lives; whether it's safety, security; whether it's someone who's getting married or someone visiting someone they haven't seen in a while or sick. We're sort of main line, main stream. But we had a micro-credit conference event here the other day, which I thought was a wonderful event. Here is a guy who started a bank and offered $50 loans. In our country, $50 loans have very little value but over in Third World countries, they make a difference to a woman who is making chairs out of reeds, whether she can go out and buy those reeds or turn to a loan shark to buy those reeds.

"It's not about General MacArthur or Herbert Hoover who was so beloved at The Waldorf…but someone who's out there trying to make a difference in the world."

So, too, have New York City hotels over the last two centuries. I hope, dear reader, you have enjoyed this "stay" at New York's great hotels as much as I have enjoyed serving as your obliging, if at times too-talkative, concierge.

CHAPTER 18

TEN BEST GRAND HOTELS

In making the following list of the 10 best grand hotels in New York I have relied only on my own instincts and tastes. No effort has been made to echo what travel editors or guidebooks have said. I have ranked them in order of personal preference with #1 being the highest, without regard to the quality of the cuisine or even of the service, although the food and service is without question excellent in all of them. This is, in effect, a "Where-I-Want-to-Be" list. I have, however, also listed a number of other hotels—to use the guidebook vernacular—that are "worth mentioning."

1. *The Plaza.* For me, these two words are the last word in grand hotels…Implicit in them are the old world charm of the gilded age of 1907 when the Plaza opened, its unsurpassed public rooms such as the Palm Court, huge, high-ceiling bedrooms and extravagantly wide corridors and "location, location, location" on Central Park and Fifth Avenue. No hotel in the world can boast as much celebrity in movies, plays, books and the media or as many celebrities who have slept, dined and gotten married at the Plaza.

2. *The Waldorf-Astoria.* This art-deco palace, boasting New York's most extensive collection of magnificent suites in its exclusive Waldorf Towers section, puts most every other hotel to shame in this regard. "The greatest of them all," as Conrad Hilton called The Waldorf-Astoria, also surpasses almost every other hotel the world over as a city within a city. Guests never need to leave its

193

limestone walls to shop, dine, be entertained by the world's greatest performers, and live like every U.S. President who has stayed
here since it opened in 1931.

3.   *The St. Regis.* Built in 1904 by John Jacob Astor IV, who went down
on the *Titanic* just eight years later, this is a jewel-box of a hotel that
has kept and even improved upon its luster in the wake of hundreds
of millions of dollars of renovations in the past two decades. It's
impossible to even walk through the hotel without feeling like royalty. Yet, unlike the Plaza and Waldorf-Astoria, which are American
counterparts of Windsor Castle, the St. Regis is more like an English or French country house. It boasts more marble and wood
paneling per square foot than most all, if not all, other buildings in
the U.S.

4.   *The Algonquin Hotel.* Though not grand in the architectural
sense—except for its two-story lobby—the hotel's literary heri-
tage as the home away from home for James Thurber, Dorothy
Parker, George Kaufman and the Algonquin Round Table and
hundreds of other playwrights, novelists and actors put it in a class
by itself. Its equally world famous Algonquin Oak Room, where
everyone from Harry Connick, Jr. to Michael Feinstein got their
starts, is one of new York's premier nightclubs in the tradition of
The Persian Room of the Plaza, Empire Room of the Waldorf-
Astoria and the St. Regis Room, all three of which have passed
into history.

5.   *The Palace.* The landmark Villard Houses, built in 1889, com-
prise some of the public rooms of the 53-story Palace on Madison
overlooking St. Patrick's Cathedral. Occupying one corner of the
nearly century old structure is Le Cirque, arguably the city's finest
restaurant.

6.   *The Pierre.* Broadway and Hollywood royalty like Richard Rodgers
and Irene Selznick have lived in this Petite Trianon of a skyscraper
hotel on Central Park. Its ballroom and cotillion room are among
the most sought after in the city for weddings and galas with guest
lists at the parties from Mariah Carey to Tony Bennett as famous as

hotel guests like John Wayne and Walter Matthau. Its service is as impeccable as its views are spectacular. Singer Kathleen Landis has no equal in singing soothing Gershwin and Hern and Arlen melodies and, when the occasion arises at New Year's Eve or other times, adds some rock to her usual classic menu.

7.   *The Essex House.* When it opened in the early 1930's it was like the real-life equivalent of a Hollywood movie set. The times have changed but the Essex House, with its art deco décor, remains an endearing and vibrant anachronism. Alain Duchass, which just may be New York's best French restaurant (as well as one of its most expensive) is located on the 58th Street side of the building and reflects the grandeur of the hotel above it, which has seen umpteen renovations and numerous owners. More raffish than regal, The Essex House still evokes a bygone illusive glamour.

8.   *Peninsula.* Built as perhaps the city's premier apartment hotel when it opened shortly after the St. Regis across the street, the Gotham, as it was originally called, attracted movie stars and society movers and shakers by the score. Its roof garden is one of New York's most romantic treasures, affording views all up and down Fifth Avenue and of Central Park. Its swimming pool and health club, too, have the grand good fortune of sweeping views of the city, inspiring awe if not more laps in the pool.

9.   *The Sherry-Netherland.* Looking like a grand fairy tale castle, complete with its towering spire, the Sherry-Netherland, is a 1920's masterpiece of architectural fantasy. Once the home of the late theatrical producer extraordinaire Lucille Lortel, the so-called "Queen of off-Broadway," and late producer Martin Kaufman, who co-produced *Grand Hotel* and many other shows, the hotel today is mostly a cooperative apartment house with some 60 rooms and suites available to transient guests. Yet with Doubles, the exclusive club located down a set of spiral stairs from the lobby, and the presence of A La Veille Russe, the purveyor of antiques from Czarist Russia, and Cipriani, the hotel remains a glamorous attraction for old and new money.

10.   *The Carlyle.* The few available suites open to the public have few, if any, equals anywhere in the world, with grand pianos, and their picture windows overlooking Central Park. Ludwig Bemelmans lived in the penthouse suite for a year when he was painting the walls of Bemelmans' Bar with his joyful animal and human creations. Fred Astaire and Ginger Rogers would have been at home dancing in the hotel's lobby with its stunning black-and-white burnished marble floor. The Café Carlyle is host to Woody Allen's Dixieland Band on Mondays and Eartha Kitt, Barbara Cook and other topflight entertainers later in the week.

Worth mentioning:

The Fours Seasons on East 57th Street is an I.M. Pei masterpiece of architecture, with the aura of grand hotels from an earlier era and huge Waldorf-Astoria-sized bathrooms and wonderful city and Central Park views.

The Regency on Park Avenue is known by entertainment insiders as "Hollywood East" for all the film stars who stay here for film work in New York and its celebrity aura is enhanced by the presence of Feinstein's at the Regency, the Big Apple's premier nightclub.

Intercontinental The Barclay New York. Ernest Hemingway squirreled away here, in this grandest of original apartment hotels, to correct galleys for a book. Today, with nearly 700 rooms (with 84 suites) the Intercontinental The Barclay is a grand hotel on an intimate scale.

The Lowell on 63rd Street. F. Scott Fitzgerald stayed here years after he was thrown out of both the Biltmore and Commodore hotels during his honeymoon with Zelda. By the 1930's when he was at the Lowell, Fitzgerald had arrived and you will feel like you have, too.

Other grand hotels I recommend:

The Mark, 25 East 77th Street
The Plaza-Athenee, 37 East 64th Street
The Ritz-Carlton, 50 Central Park South
The Elysee Hotel, 60 East 54th Street
The Chelsea Hotel, West 23rd Street
The Michelangelo (formerly the Taft), 151 West 51st Street
The SoHo Grand, 310 West Broadway, and the Tribecca Grand
The Roosevelt Hotel, Madison Avenue
The Mercer, 147 Mercer Street
Paramount, 235 West 46th Street

INDEX

BearManorMedia

P O Box 750 * Boalsburg, PA 16827

Plain Beautiful:
The Life of Peggy Ann Garner

The life story of one of Hollywood's most beloved child actors, whose performance in *A Tree Grows in Brooklyn* won her the Oscar.

$19.95   ISBN 1-59393-017-8

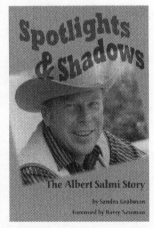

Spotlights & Shadows
The Albert Salmi Story

You know the face. You know the credit list: *Lost in Space, Escape from the Planet of the Apes, Gunsmoke, Bonanza, Kung Fu, The Twilight Zone* and hundreds more...But who was Albert Salmi?

Sandra Grabman's biography is a frank and loving tribute, combined with many memories from Salmi's family, friends, and co-stars, and includes never-before-published memoirs from the man himself. From humble beginnings—to a highly successful acting career—to a tragic death that shocked the world—Albert Salmi's story is unlike any other you'll ever read.

$19.95   ISBN: 1-59393-001-1

visit www.bearmanormedia.com
Visa & Mastercard accepted. Add $2 postage per book.

9 781593 930349